ENERGIZERS

Campus Life Books

After You Graduate
Against All Odds: True Stories of People
      Who Never Gave Up
Alive: Daily Devotions
Alive 2: Daily Devotions
The Campus Life Guide to Dating
The Campus Life Guide to Making
      and Keeping Friends
The Campus Life Guide to Surviving High School
Do You Sometimes Feel Like a Nobody?
Going the Distance
Good Advice
Grow for It Journal
How to Get Good Grades
Life at McPherson High
The Life of the Party: A True Story
      of Teenage Alcoholism
The Lighter Side of Campus Life
Love, Sex & the Whole Person:
      Everything You Want to Know
Making Life Make Sense
Next Time I Fall in Love
Next Time I Fall in Love Journal
The New You
Peer Pressure: Making It Work for You
Personal Best: A Campus Life Guide
      to Knowing and Liking Yourself
The Shocking Truth About Bowling Shoes
      and Other Bizarre Tales
Welcome to High School
What They Never Told Me When I Became a Christian
When You're on Your Own
Worth the Wait:
      Love, Sex, and Keeping the Dream Alive

ENERGIZERS

LIGHT DEVOTIONS TO KEEP YOUR FAITH GROWING

Nate Adams

A DIVISION OF CTI
CampusLife
BOOKS

ZondervanPublishingHouse
Grand Rapids, Michigan

A Division of HarperCollins*Publishers*

Energizers
Copyright © 1994 by Nate Adams

Requests for information should be addressed to:
Zondervan Publishing House
Grand Rapids, Michigan 49530

Library of Congress Cataloging-in-Publication Data

Adams, Nate.
  Energizers : light devotions to keep your faith growing / Nate
Adams.
    p. cm.
  ISBN 0-310-37371-9 (pbk.)
  1. Teenagers—Prayer-books and devotions—English. 2. Devotional
calendars. [1. Prayer books and devotions. 2. Christian life.]
  I. Title.
BV4850.A34   1993
242'.63—dc20   93-22722
                                                            CIP
                                                             AC

Edited by J. Cheri McLaughlin
Cover designed by Jamison Bell
Cover illustration by Timothy Pagaard
Interior illustrations by Timothy J. Walburg

Printed in the United States of America

94 95 96 97 98 / ML / 10 9 8 7 6 5 4 3 2

DEDICATION

To Beth, Caleb, and Noah, who love me so patiently, and laugh at the right times—usually.

————————————

To the terrific family and friends who have filled my life with both common and uncommon experiences—and forgiven me for writing about them.

————————————

To my youth group, who endured so many devotions like these—and occasionally remembered the point.

————————————

And to my Lord, who continues to take the smallest experiences of life and give them eternal significance—even when I don't notice right away.

CONTENTS

Day	Subject	Page

WEEK 1

1. A Mouthful of Moth — Temptation — **15**
2. Checking in to a Roach Motel — Sin — **17**
3. Spaghetti in Your Ear — Devotional Life — **20**
4. Laughing with Trish — Dating — **22**
5. Waiting in the Car Without Breaking the Windshield — Christ's Return — **25**
6. A Free Throw with No Time Left — God's Grace — **27**
7. Mud Between Your Toes — Praising God — **30**

WEEK 2

8. Changing the Toilet Paper — Sharing Your Faith — **33**
9. Driving the Back Roads Again — Commitment — **35**
10. Teaching the Eighth Grade—Unexpectedly — Serving God — **38**
11. A Man Falling Overboard — Repentance — **40**
12. Kissing — Friendship — **42**
13. A Drive to Des Moines — Knowing God Personally — **45**
14. Washing Your Car for Three Hours — Prayer — **47**

Day	Subject	Page

WEEK 3

15. A Klingon Cloaking Device   Parables   **49**
16. Buying Short, Fat Glasses   Avoiding Temptation   **51**
17. Making Jell-O   Peer Pressure   **54**
18. A Surprise Party   Salvation   **56**
19. Blowing Your Nose Instead of Your Own Horn   Success   **58**
20. Walking Through Danger to a Ghost   Faith   **61**
21. Rereading Your Favorite Letters   Bible Study   **63**

WEEK 4

22. A Hair Ball   Sin   **66**
23. Mandatory Roller-Skating   Faith   **68**
24. Yelling "Shut Up!"   God's Holiness   **70**
25. A Good-Looking Toilet Cake   Hypocrisy   **72**
26. Your Yearbook Picture   Your Reputation   **74**
27. A Mysterious Middle Name   The Gospel Message   **77**
28. Knowing Your Banker Personally   Assurance of Salvation   **79**

WEEK 5

29. Bad Words on the Front Porch   God's Righteous Anger   **82**
30. Enjoying a Rock Fight   Acceptance   **84**
31. A Broken Mirror and a Bleeding Ear   Love   **87**

Day	Subject	Page
32. An Uninviting Birthday Party	God's Authority	**89**
33. An Unexpected Crash	Christ's Return	**91**
34. A Class Reunion	Christ's Return	**93**
35. Building a Bomb Shelter	Sharing Your Faith	**95**

WEEK 6

36. An Old Story Told a New Way	Creative Bible Study	**98**
37. Flossing Your Teeth	Commitment	**100**
38. Stepping in Front of Your Dad	Commitment	**103**
39. An Unexpected Checkmate	Jesus' Death	**105**
40. Fishing, Not Hunting	Dating	**107**
41. Sweet Tarts, M&Ms, and Hostess Cupcakes	Marriage	**110**
42. Poison in the School Cafeteria	The Power of Words	**112**

WEEK 7

43. Shooting around by Yourself	Devotional Life	**115**
44. A Startle in the Magazine Section	Disobedience	**117**
45. Name Recognition	Friendship	**119**
46. Getting to Know Your Grandparents	Spiritual Growth	**122**
47. The Wrong Boyfriend and the Right Questions	Dating	**125**

Day	Subject	Page
48. Being the Best Man Instead of an Usher	Serving	**127**
49. The Newton Street Water Fountain	Salvation	**130**

WEEK 8

50. Being Both Nearsighted and Farsighted	Hypocrisy	**132**
51. Nicknaming Boogers	A Destructive Tongue	**134**
52. A Tug-of-War in Front of a Freight Train	Unhealthy Friendships	**137**
53. Playing for the Crowd	Peer Pressure	**139**
54. Little League Tryouts	Being Rejected	**142**
55. A Game of Duck Duck Goose	Salvation	**144**
56. Wanting to Kiss Carol	Living Expectantly	**146**

WEEK 9

57. Tombstone Tipping	Sharing Your Faith	**149**
58. A Computer Tutor	God the Holy Spirit	**151**
59. Praying for Your Stereo	Fickle Faith	**153**
60. Being Safe in the Car	Security	**155**
61. A Torn Paper Dress	Loving Confrontation	**157**
62. A Little Brother's Apology	Forgiveness	**160**
63. Hiding Under the Bed	Rebellion	**161**

WEEK 10

64. Getting to Know the "Unknown"	Caring for People	**164**

Day	Subject	Page
65. Wanting to Have "Friends Forever"	Sharing Your Faith	**166**
66. Butch Cassidy and the Sundance Kid	God the Son	**168**
67. A Family Resemblance	Devotion to God	**171**
68. Eggplant Casserole	God's Grace	**173**
69. Winning Snakes at the Carnival	Coveting	**175**
70. Losing Your Luggage and Learning to Love It	Growing Faith	**178**

WEEK 11

71. Help out of the Quicksand	God the Holy Spirit	**181**
72. Watering Down the Apple Juice	Compromise	**183**
73. A Bad Answer on a Pop Quiz	Pride	**185**
74. Baby-sitting	Helping Others Grow Spiritually	**188**
75. Ear Day	Being Teachable	**190**
76. Throwing an Eraser in Typing Class	Self-righteousness	**192**
77. Spending Your Savings Account	Holding Back from God	**195**

WEEK 12

78. A Mouthful of Toothpaste	Peer Pressure	**198**
79. Crowd Breaking	Following God	**200**
80. Partying in the Wrong Basement	Hypocrisy	**203**

Day	Subject	Page
81. Asking Freshmen the Right Question	Seeking God's Will	**205**
82. Beating the Clock, Not the Coach	Ministry	**208**
83. Walking in a Blizzard	Perseverance	**210**
84. Sunday Trips to the Dairy Queen	Worship	**213**

WEEK 13

85. Knowing the President's Phone Number	Prayer	**216**
86. Praying for Johnny Carson	Intercession	**218**
87. Playing Well at the Wrong End of the Court	Living for God	**221**
88. Hanging on the Refrigerator Door	Healthy Self-image	**223**
89. A Hayride with Judy	Sexual Purity	**225**
90. Cheating at Basketball	Sin	**228**
91. A Mountain Path Overlooking the Interstate	Living for God	**230**

INTRODUCTION

One of my favorite old jokes is about the prison inmate who was spending his first night in a new jail. After lights out, he hears someone yell, "Fourteen!" followed by a roar of laughter. Then someone else yells, "Eighty-seven!" and the place breaks up again. His cell mate explains that years ago someone passed out a book of one hundred jokes, which everyone read over and over until it was memorized by all the inmates there. Now all you had to do was yell out a number and everyone else called that joke to mind.

Thinking that was great fun, the new inmate says, "Let me try...twenty-nine!" No response. "Forty-two!" he yells at the top of his lungs. Still nothing. "What's the matter? Why isn't anyone laughing?" he asks his cell mate, who merely replies, "Some people just can't tell a joke."

The ninety-one devotions that make up this book are like that for me. If you called out "Fifty-seven—Tombstone Tipping," I couldn't help but laugh. Try "Thirty-one—A Broken Mirror and a Bleeding Ear," and it might still choke me up to the point of tears. Why? These are two of my private miracles.

What do I mean by private miracles? I mean the common experiences of life through which God chooses to reveal something of himself. Sometimes they're hilarious. Sometimes they're heartbreaking. Almost always they're humbling, as I realize my eternal, all-powerful God has chosen a mundane, seemingly insignificant part of my daily life to teach me something about his nature, and about mine.

For me, private miracles are energizing. They show me in my heart what I already know in my head—that God is faithfully involved in my everyday life and that he wants me to know him more and more intimately. Recognizing his hand at work in my personal circumstances gives me new energy to live for him, and to look with eyes of faith for the next glimpse of what he might show me.

Private miracles aren't just mine, and they aren't meant to stay private. That's why I've written this book. May my private miracles combine with God's Word to help you recognize the private miracles in your own life. And may recognizing those private miracles spark a new energy in your daily devotion to the One who truly deserves it.

Nate Adams
St. Charles, Illinois

Temptation is sort of like ...

A Mouthful of Moth

Do you ever wonder where the exact line between temptation and sin is? Do you find yourself wanting to do things that aren't exactly wrong ... but aren't exactly right?

There's nothing quite like running in a race and being in the lead. Way out in front of the pack is an exhilarating place. If you've never experienced it, you should round up some slow people and give it a try.

In the lead is where I found myself one day during an eighth-grade track meet. It was a 220-yard run, which in most places is halfway around the track. I was just coming into the second turn when I was taken with the not-so-humble thought that everyone else in the race was inhaling my dust. A slight wave of cockiness overcame me, and I decided to do what the track coaches tell you never to do—I looked back.

Yep, there were my suffering competitors, several feet behind me and straining hard. I turned back smugly to the home stretch of the race. That's when a fairly large moth flew between the upper and lower boundaries of my prematurely confident grin. It landed right on the back of my tongue, and suddenly the race was the last thing on my mind.

I began spitting, coughing, and hacking, and various moth parts escaped from my mouth with each effort. I actually remember thinking, "That was a wing! That was a leg! Oh yuck, that was an antenna!"

Once moth parts stopped coming out, the feeling of utter disgust set in. I had tasted—and almost digested—an ugly, fluttering insect. It had spent long enough in my mouth for me to dismember it, and who knows what microscopic parts or fluids might still be with me. What kind of doctor does one see for moth poisoning?

Although this all happened in a matter of seconds, I think you can imagine what happened in the race. That guy who was straining so hard in second place and two or three of his buddies passed me up, and I ended up having their dust as a main course for my moth appetizer. I lost the race—the race I was winning until then.

> *Therefore, since we are surrounded by such a great cloud of witnesses, let us throw off everything that hinders and the sin that so easily entangles, and let us run with perseverance the race marked out for us.* (Hebrews 12:1)

This verse makes a distinction between "the sin that so easily entangles" and "everything that hinders." Yet both keep us from running our best spiritual race.

If my competitors in that race had designated someone to grab my ankles or trip me at the starting line, well, I wouldn't even have run the race. That's one way to look at sin. It's debilitating. Confining. You don't even want to run when you're in its embrace.

The moth, on the other hand, is more like temptation. It was a distraction that took my attention away from the race just enough to help me lose it. If my mouth had been closed, the moth would have been a minor, insignificant distraction. It was when I "opened up" to it that the distraction became as effective as someone holding on to my ankles. And who knows? Maybe after you swallow enough moths, you acquire a disgusting, dangerous taste for moth soup.

Is your mouth open?

What "distractions" will you face today that might keep you from running your best race? Have you deliberately placed some hurdles out there yourself that make your race harder to run? Will you commit now not to turn your head and open your mouth, even when you're in the lead?

You might also take a look at . . . James 1:2-4; James 1:12-15

Sin is sort of like . . .

Checking into a Roach Motel

Have you ever made the same mistake you saw someone else make, even after seeing the hurt it caused that person?

Okay, okay, I admit it. We had roaches in the house one time. I think they crawled up the plumbing or had an inside track to the bathroom, because that's where I'd always see them. Usually it was during the middle of the night, with my eyes half open, my bladder the only part of me that was fully awake, my feet bare, and . . . ARRRRGGHH! The fleet-footed little creature would run across just enough open terrain to make my toes curl before it darted into some crack or crevice. And that hiding place was always shaped differently than any would-be weapon in the house.

Then we got a roach motel. If you've never used one of these things, it's almost worth getting a few roaches just to see it in action. They're lightweight, little cardboard boxes with narrow strips of . . . roach bait, I guess . . . and high-powered glue strips running along either side of the bait.

As I opened the package and examined my first roach motel, I wondered what would entice a roach inside it, and what possible good those little strips of glue could do. But I dutifully placed it in the bathroom—right by their impenetrable crevice fortress—

17

and at 2:00 A.M. I had my first catch. It was stuck just inside on the first of the three glue strips, wriggling like crazy, but definitely "checked in."

I started to throw the little motel away, but it suddenly hit me that catching one roach per motel would be an expensive way to solve the problem. So I decided to put the trap back down. My "guest" wasn't going anywhere, and while I didn't expect any halfway intelligent cockroach to go into the "occupied" motel, I took some delight in thinking of this creature as an intimidating example that would scare the rest of the tribe (what's a group of cockroaches called anyway?) out of my bathroom.

The next morning I was amazed to find five guests! Then eight, then eleven. I think the most I could ever fit into one motel was twenty-five or so. (Don't tell the roach motel fire marshal—we may have been over the occupancy level.) They would actually crawl over one another to get inside to the bait. I thought the middle strip of glue would be useless, because only the strips on each end would catch anything that came in. But when the outer glue strips were full, new roaches stepped on the backs of their trapped compatriots! My astute conclusion? Roaches are as stupid as they are ugly. Or are they?

To the Jews who had believed him, Jesus said, "If you hold to my teaching, you are really my disciples. Then you will know the truth, and the truth will set you free."

They answered him, "We are Abraham's descendants and have never been slaves of anyone. How can you say that we shall be set free?"

Jesus replied, "I tell you the truth, everyone who sins is a slave to sin." (John 8:31-34)

Jesus' conversation with his critics shows us that those trapped in sin don't consider themselves trapped. They're more interested in their desires (the bait, if you will) than in freedom from their condition. And they love company. Look at how Jesus' critics always traveled in packs, reassuring each other that their security was in their ancestry, or good works, rather than in the truth of God's salvation and liberation from sin.

Why do you and I wander into the sin trap time and time again? Maybe we just look at the bait and choose to ignore the glue—and the two always go together. Why don't those already caught in the trap warn us? They love the company and the perverse reassurance that the pack is growing and they're not alone. Why are we so slow to seek an escape from the trap? Our sin deceives us into believing we're in a comfortable motel— until we try to check out and can't pay our bill.

I never, ever saw a roach leave the motel under its own power. Of course, I held the power to redeem them from their trap and give them a fresh start on my bathroom floor. But remember, these were ugly, disgusting roaches. It's not like I was willing or able to do what our Redeemer did and become a roach myself.

Have you checked in?

Are you in any way stuck with a pack of others in self-destructive behavior? (Don't answer too quickly—remember, one of the characteristics of being there is not being able to admit it.) Are you willing to ask God for some truth to set you free? Are you willing to check out of any motels you find yourself in, right now?

You might also take a look at ... Isaiah 3:9; 1 Timothy 5:24

*Trying to have a consistent
devotional life is sort of like...*

Spaghetti in Your Ear

*Why is it that sometimes the harder we try, the less suc-
cessful we seem to be in developing a consistent time
with God?*

I don't like lifting weights. They're heavy—and once you lift
them up, you're supposed to put them right back down
again. It all seems so futile.

I do like playing basketball, however. One year after the season was over, my coach suggested that I devote some of the off
season to "lifting." I was a "tall guard" that he was trying to
make into a "small forward." That meant I had to bang around
underneath the basket with players under whose armpits my
head fit neatly. Usually they were tough guys who had tattoos
and spit a lot, often in my direction.

I took my coach's suggestion as an expression of concern. I
needed to "beef up" for my own safety as well as for the team's re-
bounding statistics. I had a couple of hours before dinner that
day, so I headed off to the weight room. There I found a "body
factory" full of machines and heavy metal that were intimidating
and unfamiliar to me.

No one was there to help me, and I didn't really expect to be
able to do much on my own. Nevertheless, I laid down at one machine and tried to lift what was there. No problem! I added a little more weight. Piece of cake! This was going to be easier than I
thought. I added as much weight as I could lift without difficulty,
and began lifting over and over and over again.

About an hour later, I had convinced myself I could "beef myself up" in no time at all. This routine wasn't that hard, and most
guys I had seen lifting hadn't done nearly as much as I had just

crammed into an hour. So I trotted off to the shower and then to the college cafeteria for dinner. I was starting to feel a little stiff and sore, but I was sure that was to be expected after a little workout.

If you know anything about weight lifting, you're already laughing out loud at me. Muscles are like rubber bands: when you stretch them and stretch them and stretch them, they either tear or pull so taut that you can hardly control them while they try to return to their original form. By the time I sat down to a spaghetti dinner, my arms, and therefore my fork, were out of control. I'm not exaggerating when I say one forkful hit my ear and another my forehead. It was more than a little embarrassing.

My friends at the dinner table thought I was clowning around at first. When I explained the reason for my handicap and pleaded for their help, they expressed their great compassion with raucous laughter. So with all the dignity someone whose arms are sprung springs can muster, I threw my milk over my shoulder and left. I was sore for days, and I've not been back in a weight room since.

But he said to me, "My grace is sufficient for you, for my power is made perfect in weakness." Therefore I will boast all the more gladly about my weaknesses, so that Christ's power may rest on me. (2 Corinthians 12:9)

At times I approach my devotional life in the same unrealistic way I approached weight lifting. Dissatisfied with where I am, I undertake an ambitious crash course entirely in my own strength. I go at it hard for a short period of time, find I am unable to sustain what I set out for myself, then let my discouragement keep me from making any progress at all. I'd be much better off to get some instruction from an expert, then humbly approach the task a little at a time, gaining strength as I go.

In writing to the church at Corinth, Paul expressed a similar frustration: things weren't progressing as he would have liked them to, even though he was working hard. He described a "thorn in [his] flesh" (see 2 Corinthians 12:7) that apparently limited his ministry goals from happening the way he'd planned. After asking

God three times to remove the "thorn," he received the answer that spiritual strength somehow resides in weakness.

If my own resolve to have a more consistent devotional life could by itself make me successful, my pride and dependency on myself would crank up a notch, and my sense of dependency on God for spiritual nourishment would crank down a notch. That's going in the wrong direction.

Maybe the next time you or I decide to "pump up" our devotional life to more saintly stature, we should clean the spaghetti out of our ear and approach God with genuine poverty of spirit. After all, he specializes in weaklings.

Where is your spaghetti these days?

Is your devotional life dependent on trying real hard? How are you doing? What kinds of things could you say to God today that would give him an invitation to be strong in your weakness?

You might also take a look at ... Nehemiah 6:9; Matthew 5:3

DAY 4

Honest dating is sort of like ...

Laughing with Trish

Have you noticed that the dating game can be full of unspoken feelings and behind-the-scenes gossip rather than up-front, honest communication? Have you ever had a relationship that you felt was built on complete honesty?

Trish and I were on our first date, and we didn't know each other very well. We found ourselves waiting for our pizza to arrive and not knowing exactly what to do with our nervous hands and eyes. Fortunately, she helped me out by asking about my recent election to the high school student council.

"There's so much that needs to be done at school," she began with conviction. "Why, you should see the condition the girls' bathrooms are in." (I had to admit that cleaning up the girls' rest rooms hadn't been on my list of campaign promises.)

"There are cigarette butts all over the restroom, and it smells horrible," Trish continued, feeling more and more confident that she and I at least had some common political interests to discuss. "I wonder if Dr. Martin [our principal] knows how bad the problem is."

I tried to inject some levity into the conversation by remarking that I was sure Dr. Martin had spent more time in there than I had. But Trish wasn't to be sidetracked with humor, at least not intentionally. She was on a soapbox. Then it caved in on her.

"You know, I think that you and Dr. Martin should march into one of the girls' restrooms next week and just smell the butts."

Now this was one of those split-seconds that seems to last an eternity when you're in it. She broke off her thought with the realization that she had just said something extremely funny, but a little "earthy." Not only did her words have a rather humorous double meaning, but now we both had to deal with the mental image of our distinguished principal and I marching into the girls' room and making certain... demands. It was all I could do to restrain myself even for that instant, but as I said, we didn't know each other very well, and I was afraid that if I laughed at her unintentional "bathroom humor" she might think me crude and vulgar.

Trish, however, bailed me out. After that brief, awkward pause, she threw her face into her hands and squealed, "I can't believe I just said that." We both spent several minutes laughing, and then several more minutes speculating on the details of that scene before our pizza arrived. The rest of the date went smoothly, and we both had a slight smile on our faces the entire evening.

When Boaz had finished eating and drinking and was in

good spirits, he went over to lie down at the far end of the grain pile. Ruth approached quietly, uncovered his feet and lay down. In the middle of the night something startled the man, and he turned and discovered a woman lying at his feet. "Who are you?" he asked.

"I am your servant Ruth," she said. "Spread the corner of your garment over me, since you are a kinsman-redeemer."
(Ruth 3:7-9)

For Boaz to "spread his garment" over Ruth would mean he accepted her as his wife. Of course, isolating these three verses by themselves makes this seem like a pretty funny proposal of marriage—not exactly the one you might have pictured with your dream mate, right?

One of the things that characterized the relationship of Boaz and Ruth, however, was direct honesty. When Ruth and Naomi (the mother of Ruth's deceased husband) realized that Boaz had the legal right and moral responsibility as Naomi's close family member to redeem the family land and marry Ruth, the context of their honest relationship encouraged Ruth to speak openly and boldly. She didn't play games. She didn't try to seduce him there in the middle of the night. She didn't tell her best friend to tell his best friend that she might be interested in him if he were interested in her. She leveled with him and counted on him to level with her.

Honesty is so important and rewarding in any relationship. Dating, especially, has plenty of mysteries and uncertainties already. Masking your real self in a role or reputation and making your partner guess what you truly think or feel makes the relationship a difficult maze to navigate.

Thanks, Trish, for laughing out loud at the butts in the bathroom. It let me know we could be real with each other, and that gave me great freedom to be myself.

Would you have laughed?

How high on the honesty scale are your current relationships, either with dates or with friends? Are you at all confused or uncertain as to where you stand with them because of toying and role-playing? What honest things could you say today that would unleash refreshing "realness" in your relationships?

You might also take a look at... Ruth's four short chapters; Psalm 15:1-2

DAY 5

Expecting Christ to return is sort of like...

Waiting in the Car Without Breaking the Windshield

Do you expect Jesus to come back in the next thirty years? The next thirty months? The next thirty seconds?

When we were children, my older brother and I often went in the car with my dad while he ran various errands. I guess there was less child abduction back then, because Dad would frequently leave us in the car while he ran into the dry cleaners, the post office, or the convenience store.

On one particular day, Dad needed to visit someone in the hospital. He left us in the car with his usual two instructions: Don't hurt each other, and don't hurt the car. We didn't know exactly how long he'd be gone, but we knew he could return at any time.

The next twenty minutes or so are sort of a black hole in my memory. I don't remember why my brother was in the backseat, why I was in the front seat, or what the argument was about. I do know I said something that provoked him (a bad habit little brothers tend to have) and that he felt compelled to retaliate. He planted both feet firmly in the back of the front passenger's seat where I was sitting, and gave it a mighty push.

You'd think that an eight-year-old head shattering a car windshield would result in considerable injury and pain, and at least bring some blood, but there was none of that. Just a dull thud, a shattered windshield, and a flurry of finger pointing about whose fault it was.

My dad was accustomed to finding a wrestling match or pouting feud in the car when he was gone for very long, but I doubt that he ever expected to return to a shattered windshield. The only thing more unusual than the windshield that he noted upon his return, was the quasi-angelic posture of his two guilt-ridden little boys.

> *"Who then is the faithful and wise servant, whom the master has put in charge of the servants in his household to give them their food at the proper time? It will be good for that servant whose master finds him doing so when he returns. I tell you the truth, he will put him in charge of all his possessions. But suppose that servant is wicked and says to himself, 'My master is staying away a long time,' and he then begins to beat his fellow servants and to eat and drink with drunkards. The master of that servant will come on a day when he does not expect him and at an hour he is not aware of."* (Matthew 24:45-50)

The way my brother and I waited in the car that day was a lot like the way the "bad servant" waited for his master in this parable. We began by convincing ourselves that he wasn't coming back right away. It's not that we thought he'd never come back, we just imagined it to always be a future event instead of something that could happen at that very moment. As a result, we behaved in a way that made us lose track of the fact that he was coming back at all.

In disregarding my father's parting commands, I ended up damaging the two things with which he had entrusted me: the car, and my relationship with my brother.

The Bible is clear that Jesus' return will be sudden and that his followers will be accountable. The only children likely to rejoice at his coming will be the ones that managed to live and behave as if he had never left the car.

Are you acting like your dad's in the car?

How would you describe your attitude today about Christ's return? Like a baby due in nine months—soon and certain, and you think you know about when? Like a man landing on Jupiter—probably not in your lifetime? Like World War III—possible, but boy you hope not? Or like someone who's crept into the room right now, undetected—and is just waiting to tap you on the shoulder?

You might also look at... 2 Timothy 4:7-8; Revelation 22:20

God's grace is sort of like... **DAY 6**

A Free Throw With No Time Left

Have you ever done your very best at something, only to find it wasn't good enough?

It was halftime. The sophomore basketball team I played on sat sulking together in the locker room. We were losing by almost twenty points to our arch rival. Not only had we played the first half poorly, we had played it with little energy or desire. Our cheerleaders might have called what we were missing "spirit." We had basically just called it quits.

I don't remember exactly what our coach said then, but I remember it motivated me. Maybe we were going to lose that game, I thought, but I wasn't going to settle for another pathetic, halfhearted half of basketball. Give me the ball, I thought.

The rest of the game I was on fire. Having managed only one meager basket in the first half, I poured in nineteen points in the second. Our team seemed to catch a new energy. We whittled away at that twenty-point lead. Going into the last minute of play, we were losing by only one point. Give me the ball, I thought.

With time running out, I drove up the middle of the court and was fouled. Just as the referee's whistle blew, the buzzer sounding the end of the game went off. Both teams cleared the floor to watch me attempt a "one and one" free throw—if I made the first one, I got another one. One would tie the game, two would win it.

I missed the first free throw off the back of the rim. What amazed me most about that experience was that no one seemed to remember my nineteen points that led our second half comeback. Most of my teammates wouldn't look me in the eye. I overheard my coach telling the varsity coach how disappointed he was in me. Later the varsity coach asked me how I could miss an opportunity like that to win the game. It wasn't how you played the game, it was whether you won or lost.

All of us have become like one who is unclean, and all our righteous acts are like filthy rags; we all shrivel up like a leaf, and like the wind our sins sweep us away. (Isaiah 64:6)

For all have sinned and fall short of the glory of God, and are justified freely by his grace through the redemption that came by Christ Jesus. (Romans 3:23-24)

Most of the "cheerleaders" giving you advice today would probably say that you just need more "spirit" to reach your goals and be successful. The human spirit is given a lot of credit for being able to do anything it sets its mind to.

But the Bible has a different message. It talks about our best efforts being like filthy rags and says that everyone falls short of God's standards when trying to be good enough. Even when you're really talented or really popular or really smart, you can't "earn" God's favor. Even when you score nineteen points in the second half, losing the game wipes out your best heroics.

That's where this thing called grace comes in. At the end of my self-sufficiency waits the small doorway of humility, and through it shines the welcoming light of God's grace. Exchanging my battered, independent, human spirit for a humble, dependent one brings the freedom and relief of meeting God's standards because of my relationship with him rather than by striving against impossible, holy requirements.

I had a hard time finding a consoling friend after that basketball game, but as usual I found my dad's accepting, encouraging arm around my shoulder. I knew then that he didn't mind that we—that I—had lost the game, but I didn't understand until much later that the number of "points" I scored had nothing to do with his love for me.

Are you at the free throw line?

Have you had experiences of grace apart from your relationship with God? For instance: Has a test you weren't really prepared for ever been canceled? Have your parents ever forgiven a debt you couldn't really pay back as you had hoped? Has someone ever continued to be your friend even after you'd hurt him or her? In what ways do these smaller experiences of grace help you today to picture and understand God's grace in your life?

You might also take a look at ... Romans 11:5-6; 2 Corinthians 12:9-10

Praising God is sort of like ...

Mud Between Your Toes

Does praising God come easily for you? Or is God's awesomeness sometimes more intimidating than inspiring?

Being a freshman can be tough. You leave junior high science class believing that the amoeba is the lowest form of life on the planet, only to have high school upperclassmen tell you you're wrong: freshmen are the planet's lowest life form.

My school's freshman initiation was particularly brutal. For a solid week, we freshmen had to wear humiliating things. We had to eat humiliating things. We had to do humiliating things. We began to feel that the week's objective was to humiliate us.

The climax to initiation week was a tug-of-war over "the pit." About twenty feet wide and five feet deep, this trough of terror was full of oozing, gushy, who-knows-what-else-is-in-there mud. Seniors delighted in telling us that there might be a leftover freshman corpse or two at the bottom of the pit and that we should not be alarmed if we felt something clutching at our ankles when we went in. As my five-boy tug-of-war team lined up against the varsity football team's offensive line, I understood why no one ever lived to become a sophomore without a dip into the pit.

Usually the advance hype in situations like this is the actual experience. Not this time. The pit was as reputation. It looked awful, then in rapid succession felt, and tasted simply awful. I can't remember wanti_g ___ __ _ place more quickly.

For me, the kindest moment of freshman initiation week came when a semi-sympathetic sophomore pulled me up out of the pit, and helped me sit down on a big rock to rinse and towel off. In that brief moment of empathy, he won my grateful admiration. Three days later, when I saw him in the locker room after gym class, I was still cleaning dried mud from between my toes.

I waited patiently for the Lord; he turned to me and heard my cry. He lifted me out of the slimy pit, out of the mud and mire; he set my feet on a rock and gave me a firm place to stand. He put a new song in my mouth, a hymn of praise to our God. Many will see and fear and put their trust in the Lord. (Psalm 40:1-3)

I really tried to get that mud cleaned off, but I'm not sorry it stayed in between my toes for a while. While the mud reminded me of the disgusting place I'd been, the fact that it was dried and in an obscure place also told me that it was over. I was out of the pit. I had a new sophomore friend who had taken pity on me, and I wasted no time telling everyone I could about him. He had helped me out of the pit, and on this side of its murky horror, I could look forward to the coming school year, even as a freshman.

Like the writer of Psalm 40 says, God has lifted me out of a pit, too. He's brought me out of a disgusting, dangerous place, and set my feet on a rock. That's why whenever I'm having difficulty expressing my praise to him, I always look for the dried mud between my spiritual toes. Remembering what he's done for me has a way of putting a new song of praise in my mouth. And the more people who hear it, the more sophomores like me there will be on the other side of the pit, helping lowly freshmen out of the mud.

Have you reflected recently on what Jesus did for you when he died? Does the memory of where you were compared to where you are make you want to praise him in a new way today? Do you ever feel like you've slid back into the pit? Might crying out to God and waiting patiently for him work this time?

You might also take a look at... Psalm 18:16-18; Ephesians 2:1-7

Sharing your faith is sort of like ...

Changing the Toilet Paper

How strongly do you feel about sharing your faith? Are there other, less critical matters where your passion for persuading or convincing others is stronger?

Different "causes" can inspire passion in different people. Some people are passionate about the environment or homelessness. Others have more trivial passions, like a hatred for anchovies. Perhaps the most trivial passion I've ever experienced had to do with toilet paper. That's right, toilet paper. I'm not talking about a passion for toilet paper. We've all experienced that when the last sheet pulls off the spool and the reserve supply is gone. The passion I'm thinking of is for the way toilet paper is mounted on the dispenser. Let me explain.

I was helping prepare the program for a youth rally of high school students from several churches in our area and was looking for something fun to get everybody's interest and attention before the main speaker. I had just read a magazine article reporting that, when surveyed, people were fairly evenly divided over how toilet paper should be mounted on the dispenser. Some felt strongly that the paper should be mounted so that the tissue rolled "over the top" of the spool. Others felt just as strongly that the roll should be mounted in such as way that it could be pulled from "underneath" the spool.

I was amused that some magazine had even made the effort to survey people on this subject, but decided this funny idea could be developed into a crowd breaker for our program. At the start of the meeting, I invited one student from each church to come up front and give us a sixty-second sales pitch on why toilet paper should be mounted either "over" or "under." After the presentations, the entire group (about 250 students) would vote with their applause.

My funny idea almost incited a riot. An equal mix of thunderous applause and heated boos followed each presentation. Youth groups split down the middle right where they were sitting as they realized the deep philosophical differences that divided them. One by one, the speakers returned to their seats to find their friends turned into either allies or enemies—all based on toilet paper etiquette.

> *Another man, one of his disciples, said to him, "Lord, first let me go and bury my father."*
>
> *But Jesus told him, "Follow me, and let the dead bury their own dead."* (Matthew 8:21-22)

The disciple in this passage was looking for a peaceful, convenient way to follow Jesus that wouldn't risk stirring up trouble at home. The father he was worried about burying probably wasn't dead yet, or else the disciple wouldn't have been out listening to Jesus (same-day burial in Jesus' day was required). Chances are the disciple's father objected to his following Jesus, or made it impossible in some other way. For this man, following Jesus would require a declaration of loyalty that surpassed even family relationships and responsibilities.

The high school students I invited to the platform didn't bat an eye at speaking boldly for the toilet paper procedure they believed in. They stood up to a hostile crowd to plead their case. How different would the scene have been if I had asked all of them to share their faith?

Well, maybe that's not a fair comparison. After all, toilet paper is something we live with every day. We spend some of our most private moments replacing and spinning those rolls. Years of practiced discipline convinces us of the benefits of "over" or "under."

No one could shake our belief, because we've proven our own technique over and over, day in and day out.

Then again, maybe it is a fair comparison. Maybe those same things should characterize our faith, and give us power and conviction for sharing it.

How do you feel about toilet paper?

How many things do you feel strongly enough about to stand in front of 250 high school students and plead your case? What's true of your relationship to those things that isn't true of your relationship to God? What steps could you take today that would give you more confidence and passion about sharing your faith?

You might also take a look at... Acts 6:8-15; 7:54-60; 1 Corinthians 9:16-18

DAY 9

Commitment to God is sort of like...

Driving the Back Roads Again

Has trying to obey God ever brought you the criticism of being old-fashioned or behind the times? How do you tell when to go with the new or stick with the old?

After my family moved to the fast-paced Chicago suburbs, I felt little desire to return to the small, rural town where I grew up. My new suburban high school had more people in it than my entire hometown. The new neighborhood where we lived was more affluent, the opportunities more numerous, the highways wider, and the traffic faster.

My family still occasionally drove past our old hometown on the way to my grandparents' house, but the interstate let us bypass in about nine seconds the entire community that had been home for nine years. Somehow that seemed fitting to me. Real life, I had found, was so much faster than that little town knew.

After several years of whizzing by on the interstate, my new bride and I happened to be driving back that way from my grandparents' house. A couple of miles before the exit I impulsively decided to pull off, drive through the old hometown, and take back roads to the interstate again.

My wife thought that would be fun too. She had heard me tell childhood stories of things that happened there. She commented that it would be like seeing a part of me to drive through the place where I was molded as a child. I discarded her comment with a rather sarcastic chuckle, pointing out that very little of that small town remained in me.

As we pulled up to the town's one traffic light, however, I felt that somehow this place was very much a part of me. We slowly drove the path I used to walk to school, and I told her who lived in each house. We stopped for a few minutes and visited with the elderly neighbor who used to fix our TV set. We walked the sidewalk where I learned to ride my first bike. We threw rocks in the pond where I first fished. We sat on the steps of the church where I met the Lord.

> *This is what the Lord says: "Stand at the crossroads and look; ask for the ancient paths, ask where the good way is, and walk in it, and you will find rest for your souls. But you said, 'We will not walk in it.'"* (Jeremiah 6:16)

Jeremiah's words make me think of the spot where the interstate crosses the road leading to my old hometown. Why would anyone choose the rugged, two-lane road when the interstate beckons? Life is faster, more exciting than God's "ancient paths" promise to be. The interstate is more popular, more trafficked. There I can whiz by people who won't drive as fast as me, I can drive in whatever lane I want, I can get to where I want to go quicker. The ancient paths are scenic diversions for my parents or grandparents. Give me the open highway.

But everything blurs on the interstate. There are no relationships, no memories. No elderly neighbors, no chance to throw rocks in the fishing pond. The ancient paths have meaning, value. They are a "good way." The interstate is expedient, a means to an end. It promises motion—not roots, not rest. The interstate helps you avoid stopping, slowing down, remembering, following. Those are traits of the ancient paths.

The next few hours after we pulled back onto the interstate, my wife and I talked about what it was like to grow up in that small town. We talked about my feeling of outgrowing it. Yet I couldn't escape the security and tranquility I had rediscovered in those narrow old streets, and I couldn't name many high school friends whom I could say I loved as dearly as that elderly neighbor.

The interstate flew under the wheels of my car, but once again the scenery didn't really register. I almost wanted to turn the car around, to try recapturing the innocence and peace I knew walking those old streets. Instead I had to settle for making an inner commitment that my new family and I would know that same small-town peace and permanence, even in our suburban home, by walking the ancient paths of an ever-new faith.

Driven the back roads lately?

Are there areas in your life today where you feel like you've outgrown doing what deep down you know is right? What kind of fast-lane temptations make the "ancient paths" seem obsolete? Can you think of an example from your past where the old way your parents advised turned out being wiser than the new way you wanted desperately to try?

You might also take a look at . . .
Jeremiah 18:15; Micah 6:8

Teaching the Eighth Grade—Unexpectedly

Do you feel good enough to serve God?

My eighth-grade English teacher walked into the classroom just as she always did, but something was different. She didn't say a word as she plopped her stack of books down on the big wooden desk and pointed a crooked finger at me. I sat up straight and swallowed hard, trying to come up with an excuse or apology for whatever had produced the guilt I was suddenly feeling.

Was it the time my friends and I had thrown gravel at the mean old sixth-grade teacher's house? No one knew about that, did they? Or maybe they had found out about the time in fifth grade when we skipped out of the library to go to the candy store across the street. No, no, they must have discovered that time in fourth grade when . . . I had no more time to take inventory of my grade school mischief. She turned the finger over slowly and used it to motion me up to her desk, where she stuck a hand-written note under my nose. "I have no voice today, except for you," it read. I looked at her, then back to the note for a second read, then back to her again. She wasn't kidding. She handed me a second note, explaining that she had cleared it with my other teachers for me to follow her to all her classes that day and teach English, responding only to her written notes and gestures.

"Why me?" I remember asking sheepishly, already wondering how my fellow classmates would respond to this arrangement. She frowned at having to write an extra note to me. "Because I said so!" her perfect penmanship replied. "Now let's get busy."

*Then the Lord God provided a vine and made it grow up
over Jonah to give shade for his head to ease his discomfort,
and Jonah was very happy about the vine. But at dawn the
next day God provided a worm, which chewed the vine so
that it withered.* (Jonah 4:6-7)

The book of Jonah is full of God's "appointed" servants. God
appointed Jonah to preach to the sinful city of Nineveh, but he
headed in the opposite direction. So God appointed a wind, a
storm at sea, and a great fish to get Jonah back in the right direction. When Jonah's preaching brought results in Nineveh, he
sulked outside the city and God appointed a plant and a worm to
teach Jonah about his grace and sovereignty.

Jonah's experience shows how much serving God depends on
his appointment rather than our qualifications or even our willingness. God wanted to do something in Nineveh, so he appointed various members of his creation to the task. A man, a
wind, a storm, a fish, a plant, a worm—Jonah may have the
book's title role, but each of the other appointees played a part in
the master drama that God was directing. Even at the end of the
book, one wonders if Jonah understood his appointment any
better than the worm did.

When God appoints us for service, he in effect is saying
what my eighth-grade teacher said: "I have no voice today,
except you." In spite of our protests, in spite of our feelings of
inadequacy or unwillingness, the compelling truth that God has
appointed us should overcome our reluctance. Our "why me?"
betrays our misunderstanding that we are going to do
something difficult. God's "because I said so, now let's get busy"
reminds us that, today, we just happen to be his choice instead
of a worm.

Got a crooked finger pointed your way?

Which way of serving God have you been postponing or avoiding until you felt better equipped or motivated to do it? Have
you sensed any "great fishes" spitting you back up in a different

direction than where your feelings had taken you? Can you picture your role and responsibility in a way that frees you from having to feel good enough to serve God today?

You might also take a look at ... Luke 19:37-40; 1 Corinthians 2:1-5

Repentance is sort of like ...

A Man Falling Overboard

Why is it so much harder to stop doing what's wrong than it is to start?

Have you ever thought about the way you would least like to die? I know, it's kind of a morbid question, and not something you want to spend a lot of time fretting about. I've given it some thought, though, and I've decided I'd definitely hate to drown in the open sea.

Imagine my discomfort, then, as we left Miami on a cruise ship bound for the Dominican Republic. The first night on board, I walked around the upper deck of the ship with my wife Beth, noting that only a four-foot railing separated us from the dark, seemingly endless waters of the Caribbean. That black water blended seamlessly into the clouded, starless sky, and visually speaking we could just have well been floating in space.

I remember commenting to Beth how easily one could go over the side of the ship, and that unless that person's brief scream were noted, no one would ever know they were overboard, much less be able to recover the body. At this point she looked a little nervous and suggested we go back inside.

The next day, however, we had the opportunity to take a tour of the bridge and ask questions of the ship's navigator. I found out that if someone went overboard (and was detected) the ship would immediately begin a wide turn that would bring it back to the same point in about forty-five minutes. Forty-five minutes! I was aghast! "How long can the average person tread water?"

Some longer than others, the navigator noted. A few years ago, that same ship was cruising through the middle of a storm on lookout for a woman who had fallen off her yacht around 7:00 P.M. A little after 10:00, they miraculously spotted and rescued her. She had been treading water, without a life preserver, in a fierce storm, for over three hours. I thought I would faint. That was my nightmare death. Fortunately, the other tour members suggested I might move on to a more pleasant line of questioning, or just move on.

Therefore, O house of Israel, I will judge you, each one according to his ways, declares the Sovereign Lord. Repent! Turn away from all your offenses; then sin will not be your downfall. Rid yourselves of all the offenses you have committed, and get a new heart and a new spirit. Why will you die, O house of Israel? For I take no pleasure in the death of anyone, declares the Sovereign Lord. Repent and live! (Ezekiel 18:30-32)

On the deck of a huge cruise ship, you can easily forget the speed and momentum that carries you forward through the water. The people around you are moving in the same direction, at the same speed, and aren't particularly concerned about exactly where they are or where they're going. Sin can be like that.

If sin has those same qualities, repentance doesn't promise to

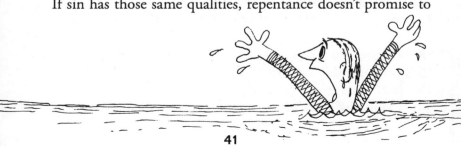

be much easier than turning the ship around. It requires an urgent warning of crisis or danger: Man overboard! The response must be instantaneous and extreme, a hard turn that may send deck chairs sliding and some passengers complaining that their pleasure cruise has been interrupted. Even after the hard turn has been initiated, it takes time to completely change directions. That change of direction is more than just necessary, however—it's a life and death matter. The man that's overboard is me, and if the ship doesn't turn around, I'll perish.

Need to turn the ship around?

As you examine your life before the Lord today, which sins have the most momentum and danger of carrying you away? If yielding to sin is sort of like a pleasure cruise, who are the passengers whose voices would try to convince you to just stay cruising? Whose are the voices of the crew that could prevail to turn the ship around?

You might also take a look at . . . Psalm 51:10-13; Luke 15:7, 10

DAY 12

Real friendship is sort of like . . .

Kissing

Who are your best friends? Is it possible to cultivate outstanding friendships, to work on them, or are great friendships something that just happen?

Kisses are memorable. I vividly remember my first, honest-to-goodness, girlfriend-boyfriend kiss, which took place on the back of a hayride wagon. I also remember one time when a girl obviously wanted to kiss me more than I wanted to kiss her—and a time when I obviously wanted to kiss a certain girl more than she wanted to kiss me. It was sort of like kissing a dead fish.

A kiss is memorable because people are vulnerable when they're kissing. Your eyes are usually closed, and even if they're open you're in too close to the person to see what their hands might do. And behind those lips are teeth.

When I kissed the girl that obviously didn't want to kiss me, I knew immediately how she felt and was embarrassed. She showed no vulnerability, and I knew I had misjudged her affection for me. That hurt deeply. No one likes to be hurt deeply. From that point on, I never kissed a girl without asking her if I could.

I don't remember many kisses that were just for "sport," without much meaning attached to them. I do remember the first time I kissed my newborn son, and the last time my dad kissed my grandma good-bye. I remember the first time I kissed the girl who would one day become my wife. I also remember the last time we kissed—just this morning.

Yes, kisses are memorable. They are often landmarks in a relationship. They can commemorate either a new level of closeness, or a new level of separation.

Jacob looked up and there was Esau, coming with his four hundred men; so he divided the children among Leah, Rachel and the two maidservants. He put the maidservants and their children in front, Leah and her children next, and Rachel and Joseph in the rear. He himself went on ahead and bowed down to the ground seven times as he approached his brother.

But Esau ran to meet Jacob and embraced him; he threw his arms around his neck and kissed him. And they wept. (Genesis 33:1-4)

Even though they were brothers, Jacob and Esau had a broken friendship. Gone were the shared childhood moments, the shared life at home, the shared experiences that bind friends together. Now Esau was riding down upon Jacob with an army of men, with every reason to take vengeance upon his deceitful little brother. Where would you begin to restore such a broken relationship? How could you hope to rebuild a friendship under such circumstances?

Apparently both Jacob and Esau recognized that vulnerability is the catalyst to friendship. Jacob bowed. Esau ran and embraced. Then came the kiss, which led to weeping and a restored relationship.

No wonder kissing has, over the ages, been an act of worship, of submission, of deepest affection. Look at what you're putting on the line—your ego, your heart, your self. No wonder some of the New Testament letters close with an encouragement to greet one another with a holy kiss. No wonder Jesus made himself vulnerable to rejection and death to show his great love for us. No wonder great friendships are so hard to come by, if great vulnerability is so hard to muster.

Ready to pucker up?

How would you rate the vulnerability present in your best friendships? Do you have strained relationships or broken friendships that could be strengthened or restored by puckering up your vulnerability and taking some risks to open up to that person? Are you waiting for them to take the first step? What would be the first step if you were to take it today?

You might also take a look at... Psalm 2:12; 1 Thessalonians 5:26

Knowing God personally
is sort of like . . .

A Drive to Des Moines

Are there times when you feel you know God well, and other times when he seems distant? Can you control that, or does God?

T he drive from suburban Chicago to Des Moines, Iowa, is not the most scenic in America. One of my best friends was getting married out there, though, and I was to be a groomsman in his wedding. My dad, who had been the pastor at the church where my friend and I grew up, offered to make the drive with me.

I can't remember a time before that when my dad and I spent six hours in a car together, just the two of us. A lot of the time was just quiet cruising, looking at corn fields. But eventually our conversation turned to my friend's upcoming marriage, my own impending graduation from college, and my dad's impressions of us boys growing up.

Hearing Dad's perspective on me as a young boy intrigued me. I began to ask him what he thought and felt when I did and said certain things. He began to ask me what I thought and felt as he tried to parent the best way he could. I began to see him more clearly as a human, struggling father, humbled by the task of raising his four kids, yet wise and capable beyond his own recognition. He seemed to see me differently, too. We laughed, debated, fought hard to express difficult things, and occasionally allowed ourselves to just sit and think.

We reached Des Moines much more quickly than I thought possible. Yet somehow I didn't want to be there yet. I wasn't ready for the drive to end.

*Jesus gave them this answer: "I tell you the truth, the Son can
do nothing by himself; he can do only what he sees his Father
doing, because whatever the Father does the Son also does.
For the Father loves the Son and shows him all he does. Yes,
to your amazement he will show him even greater things
than these."* (John 5:19-20)

One of the strongest images the Bible gives us of intimacy
with God is that of the father-son relationship. Yet in our
human experience this relationship is sometimes one of the most
underdeveloped—we may even feel estranged from our fathers.
Our ability to relate to God as a heavenly Father is bound to be
influenced by our relationship or lack thereof with our earthly
father. For the Christian, this is a compelling reason to be
rightly related to our earthly father, whatever that requires, even
if it's a one-way undertaking. I personally recommend drives to
Des Moines.

Even more important is our need for intimacy and right relationship with God, our heavenly Father. Something like a
drive to Des Moines is still a good idea. The location or destina-
tion doesn't really matter. The important thing is that it's devoted, undistracted, quality time. It's time when I ask intimate,
searching questions about character and motive. The questions
begin with who and why more than anything else. The objective
is to know the person of God, not just the activity of God that
affects me. Mysteriously, the result is that I understand more
deeply how intimately he knows me, too. And I end up loving
him even more, and not wanting the drive to end.

Been on a long drive with God lately?

How could you get away with God today? Where could you
meet with him? Could you go somewhere special, or just find a
quiet spot at home? What questions would you ask him? Can
you leave now?

You might also take a look at... John 3:35; John 14:9-26

Washing Your Car for Three Hours

Do you ever catch yourself praying for others' ears rather than for God's?

T he first day I met Beth I knew I wanted to spend more and more time with her. We had met casually in the registration line at college, and I wasn't sure when I might bump into her again. I desperately wanted to make that bump happen.

Sometimes I'm amazed at the things I've done to get what I wanted. Occasionally they were good things, like hard work, creativity, research, or saving my money. Many times they weren't so good, like stretching the truth, using people, or pretending to be someone I'm really not.

When I first met Beth, the smell of her perfume and the enchantment of her smile seemed to blur the lines between what was silly and what was reasonable. So I convinced my roommate to help me wash my car in the parking lot outside our dormitory. How would that help? The campus post office was in the lower level of our dorm. Beth lived in a different dorm, so I knew she'd eventually come over to check her mail. I didn't want to make it look like I was hanging around waiting for her, but if I just happened to be by the door washing my car....

I checked with the postal clerk and found out that mail was delivered around nine in the morning. At 8:55 on a Saturday morning, I dragged my reluctant roommate (who already had a girlfriend and wasn't nearly as motivated as I was) into the parking lot to wash my car. By 9:30 we had done a pretty good job. By 10:00 we had cleaned the inside of the car as well. By 10:30 the trunk and glove compartment had been reorganized. By 11:00 my roommate's patience was wearing thin. By 11:30 we had washed the car three more times, and he was insisting that some of the paint was starting to rub off.

"Be careful not to do your 'acts of righteousness' before men, to be seen by them. If you do, you will have no reward from your Father in heaven.... But when you pray, do not be like the hypocrites, for they love to pray standing in the synagogues and on the street corners to be seen by men. I tell you the truth, they have received their reward in full." (Matthew 6:1, 5)

Okay, so my roommate and I were hypocrites. We were standing in the parking lot, doing our "righteous act" of car washing, in order to be seen by women. Our motives were different than what we claimed them to be.

Several people passed that way several times between 8:55 A.M. and shortly after noon when Beth and her friends finally came by. I'm sure many of them thought, "He really loves that car, doesn't he?" I liked my car, but what I loved was the opportunity to be seen by someone whose attention I valued.

Sometimes that's the way I serve God. Sometimes it's even the way I pray. I'm generally committed to God, in the same sense that I was generally committed to my car. But my motive at the moment is to impress someone whose attention I value, not serve God or communicate with him. Jesus says that devalues the whole thing. My reward comes from the one whose attention my heart really seeks. Sometimes that's God. Too often it's someone else.

Whose attention are you seeking?

Whose attention besides God's might you be seeking when you serve in his name or pray publicly? How would those things be different if the attention you sought was God's alone? Would others notice the difference? Would it help to talk honestly with God about it today?

You might also take a look at . . . Ezekiel 33:31-32; Matthew 23:13-36

A parable in the Bible is sort of like ...

A Klingon Cloaking Device

Have you ever wondered why Jesus sometimes spoke in parables, rather than just saying what he meant?

D o you know any Trekkies? If you're not sure what the term means, you probably don't know one. Trekkies are die-hard fans of Star Trek. Trekkies can name any of the original Star Trek television episodes (all three years' worth). They've seen every one of the Star Trek movies (at least three times in the theater), and they also own them all on video tape. They collect an amazing assortment of Star Trek paraphernalia, and speak fluently of things like warp speed, phasers, and dilithium crystals.

Yes, if there were a Trekkie around you, you'd know it. I don't qualify as a Trekkie by a long shot, but I did enjoy the TV series, and I have seen all the Star Trek movies. Okay, maybe I'm dangerously close to becoming a Trekkie.

I doubt that the writers of Star Trek intended much spiritual truth to be hidden in their science fiction stories. In fact, Star Trek seems to glorify the human spirit and its ingenuity more than anything else. It's surprising what believing eyes can see, however, when they're focused and searching—even in a Star Trek episode.

Anyone who knows anything about Star Trek knows that Klingons are the alien race of arch enemies of Star Fleet (the good guys). At one point in their series of conflicts with Star Fleet, the Klingons developed a secret weapon known as a cloaking device. With it they could make their spaceship invisible to any detection devices, thereby making sneak attacks on other ships consistently successful.

The one drawback of the cloaking device was that the spaceship using it couldn't fire its weapons until it became visible. While the ship was cloaked, it could sneak around, but it was powerless. When it materialized, it resumed its power to attack.

The Klingon cloaking device allowed the Klingons to get close, to be right in the very presence of their enemy. From the enemy's standpoint, the Klingon ship didn't exist. Only when the Klingon ship chose to reveal itself could its enemy know both the reality and power it was facing—and once revealed, the power was great indeed.

The disciples came to him and asked, "Why do you speak to the people in parables?"

He replied, "The knowledge of the secrets of the kingdom of heaven has been given to you, but not to them. Whoever has will be given more, and he will have an abundance. Whoever does not have, even what he has will be taken from him." (Matthew 13:10-12)

Jesus used parables like the Klingons used their cloaking device. The truth contained in the parables was activated or empowered at the time of Jesus' choosing by the faith with which it was received. As long as the truth was cloaked in a parable, those who didn't believe in Jesus were befuddled. They didn't realize that parables weren't merely riddles to be figured out, but glimpses of eternal truth visible only to the eyes of faith.

The people who had hardened their hearts toward God had, in effect, closed their eyes tightly to his complete revelation in Jesus. That the parables didn't make sense to them was merely a symptom of their main disease, unbelief. By contrast, Jesus said that believers would understand the truth in his teaching and be called blessed or fortunate as a result.

The secret to the fictional Klingon cloaking device was a piece of high-tech machinery. The secret to seeing God's truth in the

Bible's parables is belief in the person of Jesus. That's actually the secret to seeing God's truth anywhere, even in "Star Trek."

Are you using your secret weapon?

Have you ever seen a card trick or other slight-of-hand trick that seemed like magic until you knew how it was done? What are other examples of mysteries that had a simple, though little known solution? Can these help you better understand how focusing on Jesus himself can unlock the Bible's mysteries?

You might also take a look at . . . Luke 10:25-37; 1 Corinthians 2:6-16

DAY 16

Avoiding temptation is sort of like . . .

Buying Short, Fat Glasses

Is there a certain temptation you seem to fall into over and over and over again? Is there anything you can do about your apparent addiction to that temptation?

When I moved into my first apartment, I equipped my kitchen mostly with extra stuff from my mother's kitchen that she didn't need, or at least didn't miss. My silverware didn't match, my pots and pans looked like they'd been used for target practice, and my drinking glasses had various cartoon characters on them—no two alike.

I didn't have a dishwasher, but since it was only me in the apartment with these simple accommodations, I often found it possible to avoid doing dishes by hand for weeks at a time. In fact, if I waited long enough, my mom would come to visit, be overwhelmed with pity or disgust, and do them for me.

One day, however, my poor dishwashing caught up with me. A friend of mine was helping himself to a drink and asked where my clean glasses were. Priding myself in the fact that I had just done the monthly dishes the night before, I told him that he could use any of the ones in the cabinet where he was looking. One by one, he picked up a glass, looked through the bottom in an attempt to see light, and placed it in the sink for me to consider rewashing.

That night as I leaned over a sink full of glasses, trying to scrub away my embarrassment, I discovered the problem. My hands were too big to reach the bottom of the narrow glasses. The sides were fine, every cartoon character was clean and happy, but the bottoms of the glasses could probably have sprouted seedlings.

From that point on, I began collecting short, fat glasses. Trying harder to reach the bottom of the narrow glasses with my big hands was futile. I needed to change my circumstances.

And though she spoke to Joseph day after day, he refused to go to bed with her or even be with her. One day he went into the house to attend to his duties, and none of the household servants was inside. She caught him by his cloak and said, "Come to bed with me!" But he left his cloak in her hand and ran out of the house. (Genesis 39:10-12)

Joseph had a boss named Potiphar whose wife was always harassing him to sleep with her. Potiphar's wife was extremely persistent, and Joseph had to live day in and day out with the temptation of letting her have her way. How did he deal with it? As much as he could, he eliminated the opportunity to be tempted. He didn't just refuse to go to bed with her, he refused even to be alone with her.

The avoidance strategy worked for a while, but when Potiphar's wife forced herself past this line of defense, Joseph had to avoid the temptation entirely by running from it. Even though Potiphar's wife lied and Joseph was imprisoned as a result, God used those circumstances and Joseph's obedience to make him the second most powerful man in Egypt, and eventually to re-unite Joseph with his family.

I had to get dirty glasses out of my house. Joseph had to get out of a dirty lady's house. The principle is the same. When you're having trouble keeping things clean in a certain setting, change the setting. If you can't change the setting, get out of it.

One final note. I have a dishwasher now, and can have any shape glass I want without fear of Mom, my friend, or the health department objecting. My ability to stay clean in that area has changed, so I have a new freedom to go back to my old circumstances. If you plan to drink something at my house, however, and happen to see that the dishwasher's broken, make sure to ask for a short, fat glass.

Having trouble keeping your drinking glasses clean?

What are the "dirty drinking glasses" you have trouble keeping clean today? Do you hope to overcome that temptation by trying harder, even though you prove yourself weak time after time? Does it show lack of faith to flee a temptation rather than let God help you handle it, or is fleeing also an act of faith?

You might also take a look at ... Matthew 26:40-41; James 1:13-15

Peer pressure is sort of like . . .

Making Jell-O

How much do your friends influence your behavior?
When they do influence you, is it good for you, or not?

When I got out of school and started living on my own, I came face to face with distasteful realities such as laundry, dishes, and cleaning the bathroom. It made me miss my mother. In fact, my new appreciation for her years of toil and labor compelled me to send her a Mother's Day card not just on Mother's Day, but every time I cleaned the bathroom. Of course, that was only two or three extra times per year, but it's the thought that counts, right?

Cooking, however, was one of those duties I couldn't easily avoid. I still remember the first thing I ever learned to cook— Jell-O. Okay, so maybe that doesn't qualify as cooking, but it does involve mixing, stirring, reading directions, and waiting. Those are basic steps of cooking, right?

Anyway, the way Jell-O works has always impressed me. You stir the mix into water that's really hot, then add water that's relatively cool, then pour it into almost anything you want. After a couple of hours in the fridge, it's ready to eat and in the shape of whatever you put it in to set.

Actually, my first Jell-O came out in the shape of our refrigerator's bottom shelf. I poured it into a plastic bowl that had a slow leak.

> *Do not conform any longer to the pattern of this world, but be transformed by the renewing of your mind. Then you will be able to test and approve what God's will is—his good, pleasing and perfect will.* (Romans 12:2)

Peer pressure is a lot like Jell-O. You take something really hot, like a mischievous idea or forbidden activity. Your emotions and adrenalin run away with the thought of it, and you start boiling with the idea of doing it, maybe just this once. Before long you're so mixed up with the notion that it almost becomes a part of you. Or you become a part of it.

Add to that the "cooling" effect of criticism or ridicule that comes if you start second guessing the idea. The looks from your friends can be chilling. The sarcastic sneers from those who aren't your friends are like icicles. You shudder at the thought of not impressing that special someone who might be part of the deal. In pours the cool water. You're feeling more and more moldable.

Then you're poured into the mold. It doesn't matter what the idea or the behavior is, because you're liquid, you'll flow anywhere, look like anything, mix with anyone. There's no room for courage or independence; they don't fit the mold. Don't think about making a stand; you'll only stick out. Jell-O settles in to one level, one color, one shape. Just relax and enjoy it. Someone else will determine what you will look like—eventually.

No! Break the mold. Don't conform to the pattern of this world, God says through Paul in the above verse. Transforming beats conforming every time, and the battleground is your mind. Transforming into Christ's likeness means setting your mind and affections on him each new day. Then you can see what God really wants for you—his good, pleasing, and perfect will. And you can bet it isn't spiritual Jell-O.

Feeling hot, cold, and all mixed up?

Who are the people who most frequently ask you to conform? What mold is their eventual goal for you? To which part of Jell-O conformity are you most susceptible—the hot temptation, the cool ridicule, or the silent settling for whatever shape they choose for you? What transforming could you do right now that would give you the courage to refuse to conform to the peer pressure that waits for you this week?

You might also take a look at ... Psalm 135:15-18; Philippians 3:8-10

Salvation is sort of like...

A Surprise Party

Have you ever thought of God's salvation plan as an unusual or mysterious thing? Was your salvation in any way a surprise?

My girlfriend and I had just gone out to dinner for my birthday and were returning to my house. It had been a pretty low-key celebration, just the two of us and dinner. Fewer people than usual, it seemed, had acknowledged my birthday. I remember thinking that birthdays received less and less attention as I got older, and that was okay... I guessed.

It just seemed funny to me that big birthday parties were reserved for little kids who probably wouldn't even know it was their birthday if you didn't tell them. We big kids, I thought, probably need birthday celebrations more than anyone. We are the ones that need a special day full of attention, pampering, and fun. Maybe that's why parents throw such lavish parties for those little kids who don't know it's their birthday. They want to throw the party they're not having themselves.

"Did you have a good time?"

My girlfriend's question interrupted my thoughts just before they plunged me into self-pity.

"Of course," I said, to help convince myself as well. "Birthdays aren't the big deal they used to be, you know."

We walked up the steps to the house, and for the split second after I opened the door, I remember thinking something was different. The room seemed, well, darker than usual and a little stuffy. I reached for a light.

SURPRISE! I literally gasped and clutched my heart at the sudden sight of thirty people standing in my small living room. Of course, my first instinct was to protect my girlfriend, but as I reached for her and looked back I saw her smiling, knowing face. She and thirty of my friends had pulled off the classic surprise party, and I had no idea it was coming.

Once I recovered from the initial shock of the unexpected birthday party, I could look back and piece together hints and foreshadowing events that pointed to the surprise. In subtle ways I had been forewarned that something unusual was going to happen, but it didn't come together for me until after I had been surprised.

And he made known to us the mystery of his will according to his good pleasure, which he purposed in Christ, to be put into effect when the times will have reached their fulfillment—to bring all things in heaven and on earth together under one head, even Christ. (Ephesians 1:9-10)

The word mystery in these verses really means "surprise" or "secret plan." It describes something that was previously unknown, but now revealed—like a surprise party.

God's plan for our salvation caught all mankind by surprise. Who would have thought God would come to earth the way he did? Who would have believed this lowly carpenter could be the Messiah that saved people from their sin? Even if some did figure out that he would "sneak up" on the world that way, who would ever have predicted that death on a cross rather than ruling on a throne would be the path to his lordship?

In the case of these verses in Ephesians, the surprise goes even further. Paul, the writer of this letter and a devout Jew himself, marvels at the fact that amidst all the other surprises, God has opened up the gates of salvation to more than just his chosen Jewish people. Christ's work makes salvation available to anyone who will come to him in faith. SURPRISE!

As I look back on my surprise birthday party, it's still easy to remember the shock and amazement I felt. It's also easy to see how everything fit together, even before the party, to make the surprise possible. But most of all I remember the fun and the joy of the party that followed the surprise.

Were you surprised?

Does God continue to work in your life in surprising ways? Should his activity in your life always be somewhat of a surprise, or does that mainly apply to salvation? Are there hints you could take note of today that God might use to direct you to the party?

You might also take a look at... Acts 15:1-31; Ephesians 3:1-6

DAY 19

Success is sort of like...

Blowing Your Nose Instead of Your Own Horn

Do you sometimes feel like the rules and standards for success are always changing? How, then, will you be successful?

While I was involved in my high school's student council, I attended a week of leadership training at a camp in Colorado. The day before I left for the camp, I started coming down with a terrible sinus infection that made my head feel like ten pounds of mucus stuffed in a tiny balloon that could pop at any minute, but wouldn't. To make matters worse, the only seat left on my flight to Colorado was in the smoking section, and the Colorado altitude only aggravated the problem. When we finally arrived at the camp, the guy from my area that I flew out with paired up with a girl and spent the rest of the week looking for chances to make out. I began viewing the whole week through puffy red eyes and cynically resolved just to endure it and go home.

To add to my misery, this whole camp was full of leader-types. Now, I myself was supposed to be a leader-type, and us leader-types aren't that bad in small doses. But a camp full of us can really be annoying. The whole week was filled with highly competitive kids lobbying to get elected, to have influence, to promote their ideas, to show they were bright up-and-comers—and I just wanted to blow my nose, preferably on one of their shirttails.

I languished most of the week, passively participating in small groups, in large groups, in group groups, and watching other leaders take the lead. On the last day of the camp, I sat in a small group that was discussing how to resolve conflict among leaders. Two really obnoxious guys were promoting two different ways of resolving conflict and were attempting to convince the group that their way was best. My head was throbbing, my patience thinning, and I interrupted their debate to tell them they were wasting our time and proving that neither of them knew how to resolve conflict. I suggested a compromise solution that would let us all get out of there early and let me go fill up a Kleenex or two.

Much to my surprise, they informed me that they had staged the whole conflict and debate to see which leaders that week had truly learned how to step in and lead in difficult situations. I had proven my leadership skills and won the hidden competition. I

rolled my eyes and snorted my disgust at their little game, then had to wipe snot off of my chin.

> *The Lord abhors dishonest scales, but accurate weights are his delight. When pride comes, then comes disgrace, but with humility comes wisdom. The integrity of the upright guides them, but the unfaithful are destroyed by their duplicity. Wealth is worthless in the day of wrath, but righteousness delivers from death.* (Proverbs 11:1-4)

This bit of wisdom from God's Word teaches that people often measure success by dishonest and deceitful means. Our natural human pride drives us to the front, to the top, to the place of leadership where we can have wealth and have our way. To please ourselves we try to please everybody, and that duplicity can make us shallow hypocrites, headed for selfish destruction.

Contrast that approach to success with God's approach, described in these verses of Proverbs. He endorses things like humility, integrity, and righteousness. These are the "accurate weights" that truly measure success. God's success is not in pressing to the forefront, but in humbly serving. It's not in pleasing the multiple standards of others to get ahead, but in doing what's right.

Apparently my sinus condition was a gift from God that week that gave me a clearer head than I might have had if I were healthy. I physically didn't feel like competing, pushing, leading, or proving myself, and that freed me to suggest what seemed right to solve the problem instead of what seemed winsome.

What's filling your head?

Do you find yourself pressing to be successful, sometimes at the expense of what's best for others or even what's right? Are you pursuing some plans right now that are based more on popular standards that will please others than on integrity before God? What would help clear your head of wrong notions of success?

You might also take a look at . . . Matthew 18:1-4; Matthew 20:20-28

Faith is sort of like . . .

Walking Through Danger to a Ghost

Are there times when faith takes you right into the face of the things you fear? Is it wrong to look for another way?

During my first year in college, I worked from 9:00 P.M. to midnight for the athletic department. My job was to monitor the racquetball courts and indoor track facilities that were under the seats of the football stadium. There wasn't much action at that time of night, so I could usually just sit and study, then walk around at midnight turning off all the lights and locking up.

The upstairs lights were easy, but downstairs there was only one main stairway leading down to the indoor track and locker rooms. That meant I had to leave one small light on at the stairway while I walked the full length of the stadium turning off the other lights. Then, with only that sixty-watt light bulb guiding my path, I walked the one hundred yards back to the stairway.

As I turned off the last locker room light one night, I found myself in complete and utter darkness. Either I had forgotten to turn on the stairway light, or someone else had turned it off. I then had to make one of those decisions like you make in the middle of the night when you need to go to the bathroom. I could turn the locker room light back on, walk one hundred yards to the stairway to turn that light back on, then walk another two hundred yards round trip to complete my job. Or I could walk in darkness—a decision that has produced stubbed toes for centuries.

It's amazing how long it takes to walk one hundred yards in

the dark. Even more amazing are the things that run through your head while you're walking. I remembered a news report from earlier that week about a chain-saw murder in our area. I remembered every teenager-slashing horror picture I had ever seen. I remembered with a fair amount of certainty that I had left that stairway light on.

> *During the fourth watch of the night Jesus went out to them, walking on the lake. When the disciples saw him walking on the lake, they were terrified. "It's a ghost," they said, and cried out in fear.*
>
> *But Jesus immediately said to them: "Take courage! It is I. Don't be afraid."*
>
> *"Lord, if it's you," Peter replied, "tell me to come to you on the water."*
>
> *"Come," he said. Then Peter got down out of the boat, walked on the water and came toward Jesus.*
> (Matthew 14:25-29)

Exercising faith sometimes means walking straight into your fear. It's hard to do. It's virtually impossible, in fact, aside from a strong commitment to reach what's on the other side of your fear. What else could explain why Peter would step out into a stormy lake in the middle of the night to walk toward what he thought might be a ghost?

Part of what drew me down my hundred yards of track in that football stadium was faith that there was a light switch at the end of my walk. The other thing that helped was keeping my feet balanced along the slightly elevated edge of the indoor track. I knew where it led, and I knew that when it began to curve I was near the stairway and the light switch.

Fear has a way of rousing religious thoughts, and I remember thinking of the psalm that says, "Thy word is a lamp unto my feet, and a light unto my path" (Psalm 119:105 KJV). In a whole new way, I saw how God's Word could be a sure ridge under my feet, even when his presence seemed distant and obscured.

Even as I reached my hand out for the light switch, I had a chilling vision of some hairy hand grabbing my wrist just before I reached my goal. Then I flipped the light on, and my entire perspective changed. Light can do that. Before I locked up for the night, I turned back to the ridge of the track, now fully illuminated for one hundred yards, and smiled.

How often do you walk in the dark?

Have you been avoiding something you know would take faith to do because of the fearful thing you'd have to walk through first? Can you visualize yourself at the end of the fearful thing, thinking it wasn't so bad? What "ridge" of security can you put under your feet from God's Word that will give you confidence as you walk today?

You might also take a look at... Hebrews 11; Philippians 1:27-28

DAY 21

Studying the Bible is sort of like ...

Rereading Your Favorite Letters

Does reading your Bible sometimes seem like a chore? What would you rather read?

I was packing up some books in preparation for our upcoming move when I spotted the old green shoe box. It puzzled me for a moment, then brought an excited grin to my face as I remembered what it was—a box of personal letters I had tucked away. I felt like a little kid whose mom just found his favorite, long-lost toy behind the couch. I opened the box and started reading.

Some were letters from former girlfriends. Others were letters from my parents or grandparents at key times in my life. There were letters from close friends who were now distant, and from distant friends who were now close. Some of the authors were no longer living. Others were no longer friends. I kept reading.

Into my mind and heart poured names, events, and relationships I hadn't thought about for quite a while. My emotions raced through highs and lows as I remembered the time of my life each letter chronicled. Sometimes I felt like I was reading someone else's mail, like those words were written for someone very different from me. At other times the words reminded me keenly of who I had become as a person, and how those very words had helped mold or scar me into my present image.

Many of the letters were painful past history, and very difficult memories to confront. I bit my lip as I read them, and marveled that I had come through some of those things without being institutionalized. Other letters were literally words of life. They were encouraging, motivating, buttressing words from people who loved me, from people who still love me.

For even if I boast somewhat freely about the authority the Lord gave us for building you up rather than pulling you down, I will not be ashamed of it. I do not want to seem to be trying to frighten you with my letters. For some say, "His letters are weighty and forceful, but in person he is unimpressive and his speaking amounts to nothing." Such people should realize that what we are in our letters when we are absent, we will be in our actions when we are present.
(2 Corinthians 10:8-11)

During New Testament days, letters played an especially important role. Because you couldn't drive or jet all over the world like you can today, letters were often used to establish the authority and intent of the person who couldn't be present. As a result, a letter could wield unusual power. It could bring tremendous consequences and was handled carefully.

Letters can still hold that kind of authority and impact, for they still represent the very person of the author. Picture someone opening a letter from the IRS requiring a tax audit or a notification that they've inherited a million dollars or a summons to jury duty. Letters can change your plans. Picture someone opening a first valentine from "the one" or a repentant note from an estranged family member or a good-bye letter from an unfaithful husband and father. Letters can change your life.

Letters say in someone's absence what that person would say if she or he were physically present. No wonder God gave us so much of the New Testament in letter form. His Word is for us a love letter, a letter of authority, a summons, an announcement of good news, and much more. In God's Word I find his very Person and the truest reflection of my own person, just as I did in that old green shoe box.

Have you opened the old shoe box lately?

Have you thought of your Bible as God's letter to you? In recent days have you found it to be a love letter, a painful reminder of where you've been, clear instructions on where to go, or something else? Would it help to write him a letter today?

You might also want to look at . . . Galatians 1:1-12; Philippians 1:1-5

Sin is sort of like...

A Hair Ball

Do wrong choices in one area of your life ever lead to wrong choices in other areas? Does sin seem to "accumulate" over time, or is it more like "hit and run"?

I have a friend whom I can make nauseous, just by speaking a few words. I don't know why I take such satisfaction in that power—and I rarely use it—but it's kind of fun to know I can always do it to her if things ever get slow at a party.

Please don't misunderstand. I don't have to say anything crude, gross, or hurtful to get to her. The subject that makes her ill almost on the spot is, simply, hair balls.

In case you don't have mammals as pets in your house (excluding younger siblings, of course), let me explain. Furry creatures such as cats clean themselves by licking their fur. We all know that. Sometimes fur comes loose. We all know that. When fur comes loose during the licking process, it can be swallowed by the animal, over time creating a hair ball in the animal's throat. One too many hairs can gag the animal, forcing it to cough up the entire, amalgamated mess. And presto! A hair ball.

Apparently it's not just the sight of a hair ball that sickens my friend. The sound that produces one is pretty revolting to her, too. If I start graphically describing a hair ball and then start making the right noises in the back of my throat, I can conjure up an image of total disgust. In fact, what you've just read would probably have made my friend gag.

But each one is tempted when, by his own evil desire, he is
dragged away and enticed. Then, after desire has conceived,
it gives birth to sin; and sin, when it is full-grown, gives birth
to death. (James 1:14-15)

Sin seems to be a process that works like the creation of a hair ball. It's gradual at first—a lick here and a lick there. No individual lick seems that severe. No individual hair seems to bear much consequence. There's this accumulation going on, however. Any one of the hairs could gag you, but the fact that they haven't so far doesn't mean hair ball day isn't coming. Hairs give birth to hair balls, and when hair balls are full-grown, they give birth to gagging.

So what do we do? Perhaps we could stop licking. That might be the equivalent of not being tempted by our own evil desires. But the Bible teaches that Christians still battle an internal nature of sin. Not being tempted would be as contrary to our nature as not licking would be to a cat.

One of many differences between us and the cat is that God has given us an escape hatch, a side exit in the process called confession. When we confess to God that we've embraced temptation and agree with him that we've sinned, he cleanses us from the dirty stuff we've "picked up" in the process, and takes away the accumulated damage. Yes, we still taste hair from time to time, even during our best efforts to "stay clean." As we check those desires and confess those failures to God, though, he helps keep them from building up and choking off our relationship with him.

Are you risking a big choking?

Are you "accumulating" any sin that you haven't talked to God about and admitted as wrong? Have you suffered any consequences yet? Can you look ahead to see how that process could "hair ball" on you? Will you tell God about it now before it chokes off your relationship with him any more?

You might also want to look at... Psalm 51:1-4; 1 John 1:9

Mandatory Roller-Skating

Have you ever tried to live by faith and yet found yourself totally out of control? Was being out of control good or bad for your faith?

I hate to roller-skate. I don't hate roller-skating as an activity when someone else is doing it. In fact, I enjoy watching a graceful skater as much as the next person. I just hate to roller-skate.

I have reasons, of course. I was usually in sports of some kind at school, and especially in the winter our basketball coaches warned us away from any activities that might result in sprained ankles or twisted knees. Consequently, I never learned to ski, ice-skate, or roller-skate. I also had a bad experience in early high school when my beautiful first date skated circles around me with another guy while I hugged a safety rail. So I should hate roller-skating, right?

Imagine my dismay, then, when the youth group I was leading at church kept pressuring me to arrange a roller-skating night. I gave them all my excuses and begged off for months, but they persisted. Finally I agreed we could go if I didn't have to skate. They moaned at the compromise, but agreed.

As I stood on the sidelines remembering the last time I had leaned on that safety rail, I noticed that the floor was clearing. I presumed there was going to be some special type of activity for skilled skaters. Suddenly I felt the strong hands of large guys lift me up off the floor and carry me to the center of the rink, though I was kicking and screaming all the way. While about fifty of them pinned me down, two of them laced a pair of skates on my feet. Then, as quickly as they had come upon me they were gone, and I faced a partly cheering, mostly jeering crowd alone, in the center of the rink.

"Lord, if it's you," Peter replied, "tell me to come to you on the water."

"Come," he said.

Then Peter got down out of the boat, walked on the water and came toward Jesus. But when he saw the wind, he was afraid and, beginning to sink, cried out, "Lord, save me!"

Immediately Jesus reached out his hand and caught him. "You of little faith," he said, "why did you doubt?"

And when they climbed into the boat, the wind died down. Then those who were in the boat worshiped him, saying, "Truly you are the Son of God." (Matthew 14:28-33)

I guess my fear in the middle of that roller rink was nothing compared to Peter's as he realized he was walking on water in the middle of a nighttime storm. All the same, neither of us had much security under our feet, and I can almost relate to his nose dive from controlled faith to desperate panic.

There's no doubt that Peter's faith lapsed at a critical time. Jesus said that was the case. But that's the middle of the story—don't miss the beginning and the end. The beginning reminds us that Peter was trying to walk in faith. He took steps that no one else in the boat did, and for a while his faith was overcoming gravity itself. Yes, his faith took a fall, but look at the result when Jesus helped him back into the boat. Others worshiped Jesus.

Back in the middle of the roller rink, I was forced to sit in my humiliation for a few seconds. Then I got up, caught my balance, and awkwardly clunked a few rolling steps to the sideline. The jeerers turned to cheerers, and the cheerers cheered louder.

Keeping strong faith sustained all the time is ideal. Faith and falling, however, is infinitely better than staying in the boat. Maybe people need to see more Christians trying, falling, and being helped by Jesus. It might even help them get in the boat and worship him themselves.

Getting your feet wet?

Have you lost control recently in your walk of faith? How did you handle it? More importantly, how did you let God handle it? If the uncertainties disappear, does the faith also vanish? Is it better to have believed and fallen than never to have believed at all?

You might also take a look at . . . Matthew 5:16; 2 Corinthians 12:9-10

God's holiness is sort of like . . .

Yelling "Shut Up!"

Since God expressed such love to us in Christ, should we still "fear" him?

My church is rather laid back and informal. Before our worship services start it's not unusual to hear a pretty loud rumble of conversation and laughter as people come in and greet one another. Occasionally, it even takes a little work to get our attention when it's time for the service to start.

This somewhat irreverent habit never bothered me when I was one of the talkers and laughers. I had heard our instrumentalists say they felt frustrated playing the piano or organ prelude over the din, and I could understand why those trying to lead the service would like more of our attention. It wasn't until I was asked to lead the congregational singing, however, that I saw how tough it was to get people's attention off of their conversations and on to God and his worship.

On this particular Sunday night, the pleasant summer weather and church softball game that afternoon had put people in a particularly festive mood. The instrumentalists had completed the prelude, and I was standing at the microphone waiting for the noise to die down. It didn't. I cleared my throat into the microphone, but there was little response. Many people were still engrossed in conversation and hadn't even turned around to face the front yet.

I don't know what came over me. It was with a half mischievous, half serious, but quite loud voice that I leaned into the microphone and yelled, "SHUT UP!" It actually came out a little louder and harsher than I expected.

Jesus entered the temple area and drove out all who were buying and selling there. He overturned the tables of the money changers and the benches of those selling doves. "It is written," he said to them, "'My house will be called a house of prayer,' but you are making it a 'den of robbers.'" (Matthew 21:12-13)

I got a lot of shocked looks when I yelled "shut up" in church, but I didn't turn over any pews or spill the offering plates like Jesus did. I was a little annoyed at not having the congregation's attention. Jesus was righteously angry in the way only God can be.

This same Jesus who held children on his lap, proclaimed peace and reconciliation, healed and helped people was turning over tables in the temple area! Apparently it's not inconsistent for a loving, forgiving God to demand reverence rather than raucousness in the place set aside for prayer and worship. Apparently the nearness and intimacy he has given us through Jesus does not change the majesty and holiness of his character.

After about three seconds of hushed silence, the yackity worshipers at my church laughed their relief. It was just me, and I was just joking. But my spontaneous shout had startled all of us a little—myself included. I think there was a brief realization by all of us that we were in a place where "shut up" isn't usually yelled, where tables aren't usually overturned, and where neither should be necessary. I wonder if those three seconds weren't the most legitimate worship we experienced that evening.

What would get your attention?

When was the last time you felt in awe of God's holiness? Did something happen to draw your attention to his majesty? Do you find it easy to presume upon God's friendship and forgiveness? Do you need to "shut up" for a minute today before approaching him in prayer?

You might also take a look at . . . 2 Samuel 6:1-7; 2 Chronicles 26:16-21

Hypocrisy is sort of like . . .

A Good-Looking Toilet Cake

Do you know people who act one way on the outside but occasionally show a different character on the inside? Has anyone ever called you a phony or a hypocrite?

Our church has an annual "Men's Cake Bake." It was never an event that held much fascination for me, but one year a guy in our youth group convinced me it would be fun to give it a try. We knew we had little or no chance for the "best tasting" or "best looking" award, but we decided we could at least try for the "most creative" award, usually given for the cake "sculpted" into the most unusual shape or size. In previous contests, men had baked cakes and shaped them like flowers, spaceships, animals, even like a roll of Lifesavers candy.

We decided to make a toilet cake. Two 13" x 9" cakes standing on end formed the "tank" of our toilet cake. Three round cakes stacked in front of the tank formed the "stool," once we hollowed out the middle and inserted a small, plastic mixing bowl. We wrapped a handle in aluminum foil and attached it to the tank with toothpicks. Inside the mixing bowl we poured blue-colored water and added miniature Tootsie Rolls. The entire cake was iced over with white, porcelain-colored icing. The cake, of course, was chocolate.

Unfortunately, our cake was too moist and fragile. By hollowing out the middle of the round cakes, we had undermined its structural stability. By the time we arrived at the contest, our toilet cake was cracked and falling apart. A quick-minded lady at church, however, saved the day for us. First, she sent me down to the grocery store to buy some white, whipped topping. Then she bundled the whole cake up in clear plastic wrap, iced it over with the whipped topping, and put it in the refrigerator to "set" for a few minutes before the contest.

When it came out of the refrigerator, our toilet cake was a mess on the inside, but the outside looked good enough to sit on. We didn't win "most creative," but the judges were good sports and instituted a new award in our honor. We won "most unusual" cake, hands (and lid) down.

> "Woe to you, teachers of the law and Pharisees, you hyp-
> ocrites! You are like whitewashed tombs, which look beauti-
> ful on the outside but on the inside are full of dead men's
> bones and everything unclean. In the same way, on the out-
> side you appear to people as righteous but on the inside you
> are full of hypocrisy and wickedness." (Matthew 23:27-28)

A toilet cake sounds pretty gross until you start reading Jesus' words describing the religious leaders of his day. Rotting graves with whitewashed tombstones form a rather graphic picture of hypocrisy. Cemeteries are actually quite tranquil and beautiful on the surface. So are toilet cakes.

As my friend and I dug in to eat our masterpiece after the contest we betrayed its polished looking exterior. We pulled out only a few spoonfuls of chocolate cake before we ran into plastic and spilled blue water and soggy Tootsie Rolls. It wasn't really fit to eat, though as a cake that should have been its primary purpose.

Putting a right-looking, polished exterior on interior corruption and ugliness doesn't work for long with anybody, and it doesn't work at all before God. Jesus' eyes penetrated the religious leaders' facade quicker than our spoons penetrated our toilet cake. What we saw was ugly and useless. What Jesus saw was deceptive, dangerous, and bound for harsh judgment.

Does your icing match your cake?

Do you sometimes find yourself pretending to be more "spiritual" so people will be impressed with you? Does it work? How does it go over with God? Could your spiritual cake bake a little longer today before you ice it for the world to see?

You might also take a look at . . . 1 Samuel 2:3; Psalm 51:5-10

DAY 26

Your reputation is sort of like . . .

Your Yearbook Picture

How would you describe your reputation? Is it different with your friends than with others who don't know you very well?

Have you ever noticed that schools often choose the worst possible day to take photographs for the yearbook? Inevitably, your complexion waits until picture day to pop out the year's largest and most unsightly zit. Of course, Mount Pimple isn't content to be on the back of your neck or under your chin. It wants to be front and center, where the camera's flash can illuminate and magnify it, leaving your classmates to wonder if you have two noses.

If it's not your complexion, it's your hair. If it's not your hair, it's your clothes. And if everything adorning your body is in perfect shape that day, you can count on the camera's flash catching the goofiest facial expression you've ever conjured up, complete with closed eyes.

I paged through one of my yearbooks recently, and after cringing at my own picture I began glancing through those of my classmates. Each photograph brought to my mind its own snapshot of a memory. There was Joe, the football player who sat next to me in typing class. He'd begin every class by smashing his fist into the keyboard of his manual typewriter to see how many of the keys he could get to stick down. Then there was Bob, the young man from my gym class who had absolutely no sense of personal hygiene. The tragic fate of alphabetical order always put Bob by my side in gym class, and wrestling matches always put his armpit near my face. Looking at his picture, I realized I'd always remember Bob more as an odor than a personality.

Ah, but then there was Jan from my French class. She was poetry in motion and beauty personified. I used to go through the whole morning just day-dreaming about the few minutes I'd get to sit and listen to her tongue roll off French words. What powerful memories her picture still commands.

I looked at several other pictures that way, and realized that in almost every case my relationship to that person had been reduced to one impression, one summary statement of their personality and character. It made me wonder what they would think today if they looked at my picture.

Enoch walked with God; then he was no more, because God took him away. (Genesis 5:24)

Sometimes the Bible tells a great deal about someone. Abraham, Moses, David, Peter, Paul. We can feel like we know them a little because we have lengthy accounts of their behavior, their words, their lives of faith.

There are also many people whom the Bible introduces very briefly. We have only a snapshot, only a handful of inspired words to summarize years and years of living. Take Enoch for example. The summary statement of his life was that he walked with God.

That's what a reputation is—a snapshot that summarizes the personal character you've built and earned over a period of time. I'm sure Bob has learned to wash his socks by now, and that Joe uses a word processor instead of a typewriter (though he may still type with his fist). Jan probably doesn't remember a word of French, nor would she captivate my attention as she once did. Each one has probably built a new life, a new reputation with the people around them now. But they can't escape the reputation they earned with their high school peers, and my snapshot of them will always be the same. As I realize what their snapshot of me must be, I find myself wishing it could be more like Enoch's and less like the one in my yearbook.

How does your picture look?

What percentage of your reputation would you say has to do with your relationship to God? Do others know that you know him? How much of your reputation should God be? How do you want to be remembered ten or twenty years from now when your classmates are looking through their yearbooks and see your picture? Do you need to do something today to start building that type of a reputation?

You might also take a look at ... Matthew 5:16; Acts 10:1-2

The gospel message is sort of like . . .

A Mysterious Middle Name

Does it concern you that your faith makes sense to you, but not to so many intelligent people around you?

I have an unusual middle name. When people ask me what it is, I usually invite them to guess and offer to give them the first letter as a clue. Most folks feel having the middle initial makes it a fair game, and are sure they can guess their way to any name in ten or twenty tries. No one's ever guessed mine with only that hint. My middle initial is Y.

The most fun I ever had with that unusual middle initial was during my first week at a new job. The lady who files tax and insurance forms called me and asked me what my middle initial was.

"Y," I replied.

"Well, because I'm filling out these tax forms, and it asks for your middle initial," she replied.

"Y," I repeated.

"I don't know WHY," she insisted, "that's just the way the form is. Now what is it?"

"Y!" I insisted, realizing by now that she was misunderstanding me, but having too much fun to put her out of her misery.

"Look, when you get ready to tell me, you give me a call," she snapped. Click. She didn't find the mystery game I was playing at all amusing, and she didn't realize that the answer to her question was right under her nose.

For the message of the cross is foolishness to those who are perishing, but to us who are being saved it is the power of God.
(1 Corinthians 1:18)

Have you ever been the only one in a group who didn't get the joke or didn't understand how something works? Ever been the one to know the answer and watch others get frustrated at being left on the outside? For the one who doesn't understand, the mystery isn't amusing. It's confounding and confusing.

The gospel—the way God has chosen to restore us to a right relationship with himself—makes no sense at all to people who don't know him, even intelligent people. It's nonsense. Foolishness. They don't get it at all. That shouldn't surprise us. If a right relationship to God could be figured out, it would be a work of man's logic and intellect, and he'd praise himself for figuring it out, rather than praising God for doing it in a mysterious, miraculous way that depends wholly on his own standards and character.

By the way, when I went down to that lady's desk and explained the difference in my "Y" and her "why," she got a big kick out of it. Another lady was walking by, and she pulled her over and insisted that she ask me what my middle initial was. Dutifully, this second lady went through the whole routine again while the first lady grinned knowingly. She was having fun now, because she knew. There's something about knowing the secret, about having experienced the mystery, that makes you enjoy telling others, and delighting as the "foolishness" is revealed to them too.

Have you got a secret?

Do you ever think of the gospel as this incredible, neat, mystery whose secrets have been shown and entrusted to you? How does faith in God rather than dependence on self unlock the mystery? Who might you let in on the mystery today, and how might you do it?

You might also take a look at . . . Matthew 13:44-46; Colossians 1:24-2:3

*Assurance of salvation
is sort of like . . .*

Knowing Your Banker Personally

Do you ever catch yourself wondering if God has really granted you the salvation and eternal life you're counting on?

My first savings account was at the only bank in the small town where we lived. In a town that size, most everyone knows everyone. So when we walked into the bank to deposit my first five dollars, I knew my banker and he knew me.

It wasn't easy to give him my money. Prior to that time any money I ever had was kept securely in my cowboy billfold—safe, secure, and ready to be spent on a moment's notice. Now it was in this large, austere, quiet building with bars on the windows. It didn't seem nearly as secure as in my cowboy billfold.

In my cowboy billfold, my money was always near me. I had complete control over it, and could draw on my treasure whenever I wanted, for whatever reason I chose. And safe? You should have seen the zipper that sealed my genuine cowhide vault. Who could convince me that a bank was more reliable and beneficial?

My dad could. He was the one who introduced me to the concept of banking. He had a bank account himself, he said. He knew the banker personally. He knew it would be safer there than in my cowboy billfold. Furthermore, the bank would do something for me my cowboy billfold couldn't promise to do—it would pay me interest.

And of this gospel I was appointed a herald and an apostle and a teacher. That is why I am suffering as I am. Yet I am not ashamed, because I know whom I have believed, and am convinced that he is able to guard what I have entrusted to him for that day. (2 Timothy 1:11-12)

The trust that it took for me to walk out of that bank with an empty cowboy billfold is not unlike the trust I've placed in Jesus Christ. There's something awesome, holy, and austere about God that makes me want to stay out of his presence and keep my life and my treasures to myself.

One day, however, someone who knew Jesus personally walked me into his presence and told me he is trustworthy. And once I had met him myself, I was convinced that my life was far safer in his possession than it could ever be in mine.

During difficult times it's easy to feel like clearing out your account. In fact, there are people who feel that under their mattress is a safer place than in a federally insured bank. It all boils down to trust, and trust comes from knowing your banker personally.

Sometimes I'd walk into that bank with no deposit or withdrawal, just to ask about my money. My patient banker would smile, check my account, and pencil in the interest I had earned in my little savings passbook. Then I'd walk back out into the sunshine, knowing my investment was safe, and that I had daily interest to prove it.

Time to check in with your banker?

Do you tend to neglect or doubt your eternal security more during good times or tough times? Do those doubts come when you're spending a lot of time with God or a little time? How eternally secure do you feel today? What evidences do you see in your life that he's "paying interest" on your investment with him?

You might also take a look at ... Philippians 1:3-5; 2 Peter 3:8-15

God's righteous anger is sort of like ...

Bad Words on the Front Porch

*Does God still get angry? What makes him angry?
Should your anger be like God's?*

When I was a young boy, I had a treasure box. Actually, it was an old metal tackle box, and the things in it were treasures to me only: my baseball cards, a pocketknife, a bag of rubber bands, a couple of neat rocks I had found, and a few other personal items.

One summer morning I was rearranging the treasures in my box. (They really didn't need rearranging, but what else does a young boy do with treasures like that except admire them and move them around?) My older brother, bored and looking for mischief, reached into the box and took my little bag of rubber bands.

"Give those back!" I screamed, in a tone that of course only delights and motivates older brothers. Would you believe he apologized sweetly and returned them to me? Of course you wouldn't. He ran out the front door of our house with them in his hand, taunting me and making fun of my "stupid" treasures.

I followed him out the front door and onto our big front porch, but I had no hope of catching him. For that brief moment, I forgot that we lived next door to the church where my dad was the pastor. I forgot there was a wedding at the church that morning.

What I remembered was every word of profanity I had been hearing at school for the past several months, and finding no other weapons at hand, I hurled those words at the top of my lungs. I didn't know what they all meant, and they probably didn't make a lot of sense the way I used them. But there they were for every wedding guest on the front lawn of the church to hear coming from the pastor's front porch. The next thing I remember was my mother's hand slapped over my mouth as she dragged me on my heels back into the house.

He is the image of the invisible God, the firstborn over all creation. For by him all things were created: things in heaven and on earth, visible and invisible, whether thrones or powers or rulers or authorities; all things were created by him and for him. He is before all things, and in him all things hold together. And he is the head of the body, the church; he is the beginning and the firstborn from among the dead, so that in everything he might have the supremacy. For God was pleased to have all his fullness dwell in him, and through him to reconcile to himself all things, whether things on earth or things in heaven, by making peace through his blood, shed on the cross. (Colossians 1:15-20)

Christ's role as creator gives him right of ownership over all his creation. It's his treasure, just like the baseball cards and rubber bands were mine as a boy. It is God's intent that Christ be supreme over all things, seen and unseen, because they were created to honor him.

But there is a thief who would steal as much as he can from Christ's treasure. He lies, deceives, runs, taunts. And when Christ is separated from part of his treasure, his anger at the separation is righteous, just, holy, and motivated by love for that which has been lost. It's the anger of a creator and owner who has been robbed.

That's why the Old Testament tells about God causing earthquakes that swallow people. It's why you see Jesus turning over money changers' tables in the temple. God's anger is always at sin, because sin separates owner from treasure. The price of returning treasure to owner was the owner's own death on a cross.

Unfortunately, as a boy, I expressed my righteous anger in an unrighteous way. But my mom was there to express her own righteous anger with the behavior that threatened her treasure of a son. And that treasure of a son can still taste the soap in his reclaimed mouth.

Hear any angry words from the front porch?

How is God's anger different from the anger you feel? How is it the same? Are there any current world events in which you sense God's anger? Are there any events in your personal life where you sense God's anger toward known sin? What would it take to bridge the sin and return the treasure to its owner? Are you ready to tell God about it now?

You might also take a look at . . . Numbers 16:22-38; Matthew 21:12-13

Acceptance is sort of like . . .

Enjoying a Rock Fight

Whose acceptance do you really crave? Is the need to feel accepted a positive thing or a negative thing?

My older brother wasn't always nice to me when we were growing up, and I wasn't always nice to him. But there were occasional, hopeful glimpses of brotherly love between us. Deep down we wanted each other's respect and acceptance, but sometimes with brothers there is a delicate balance between love and hate, between friendship and enmity, between fun and danger. A brother can sometimes be the closest source of either peer acceptance or harsh rejection.

I thought maybe my brother and I were going to have one of those moments of acceptance when he invited me to come outside and play with him. My parents were inside visiting with my grand-parents, and since we couldn't go anywhere or have any friends over, my brother was bored. I didn't care why he wanted to play with me or what he wanted to play. I was just excited to do anything with my big brother that he wasn't being forced to do.

I was about eight, and he was ten. Behind our house was an alley filled with fairly large rocks, most of them between the size of a golf ball and a baseball. My brother led me out there and in-troduced me to a game he called "target practice." It was a simple game. We stood about twenty feet apart and took turns throwing rocks at each other. The object, he said, was to see how close we could come to each other without actually hitting each other.

Apparently, I was better at the game of missing than he was. A few minutes later I had blood gushing from my forehead, my brother was in deep trouble, and I didn't care as much if he accepted me anymore.

A man was there by the name of Zacchaeus; he was a chief tax collector and was wealthy. He wanted to see who Jesus was, but being a short man he could not, because of the crowd. So he ran ahead and climbed a sycamore-fig tree to see him, since Jesus was coming that way.

When Jesus reached the spot, he looked up and said to him, "Zacchaeus, come down immediately. I must stay at your house today." So he came down at once and welcomed him gladly.

All the people saw this and began to mutter, "He has gone to be the guest of a 'sinner.'" (Luke 19:2-7)

Like so many needs and desires God has created within us, the need for acceptance is something good that we corrupt into some-thing bad. It's natural to want acceptance. Our desire to be ac-cepted by God leads us to recognize our sin and turn to Christ as the only channel of acceptance. In turn, feeling accepted and for-given by God frees us to accept and forgive each other.

The problem comes when we seek acceptance from others as a

substitute for acceptance by God. I wanted to be accepted by my brother to help me feel good about myself. If that meant letting him throw rocks at me, fine. The desire for acceptance clouded my judgment and led me into behavior that was self-destructive.

Zacchaeus' sin separated him from God. He was enslaved to greed and corruption, and his judgment was clouded as well. He spent his life cheating the people in his crowd, then hopping around on the outside of their acceptance trying to see inside.

It wasn't until Zacchaeus sought acceptance from Jesus that he saw clearly why his wealth didn't give him peace or gain him acceptance by others. When Jesus accepted Zacchaeus, he was immediately freed to do what was right in his other relationships. Then, whether the crowd accepted him or not, he knew he had done what was right before God and toward others, and that their rocks of rejection couldn't hurt him anymore.

How many rocks will it take?

Are you seeking acceptance from a person or a group without feeling truly accepted by God? Would feeling truly accepted by God for who you are in him change how you feel about needing others' acceptance?

You might also take a look at... Micah 6:6-8; Ephesians 2:8-9

A Broken Mirror and a Bleeding Ear

Is there someone you love so much that their death would debilitate you, cripple you with grief? What would it be like to choose for that person to die so that someone else could live?

There was a nineteen-month period during which I had an "only begotten son." I can't adequately explain what it's like to be a father with an only son. It's as if your whole focus shifts from yourself and your spouse to this one that is made in your very image. Things that you thought you'd never do or give up for anyone don't seem to matter as much any more. He's the apple of your eye, the subject of your deepest interest. You get incredible enjoyment just from watching him sleep.

I was shaving when I heard the crash. In that millisecond that it takes to react to a loud noise, a dozen things raced through my mind; the heavy, full-length mirror that was leaning against the wall of our bedroom had stayed there much too long; I should have mounted it to the back of the door as I had intended weeks ago. But even if it fell, it wouldn't have broken on the carpeted floor, would it? Where is Caleb? Should I have been watching him? Where is his mother? Surely our little one-year-old couldn't have budged that heavy mirror ... could he?

Then I heard Caleb's scream. I flew around the corner to see a zillion pieces of broken mirror on the floor, and Caleb laying in the middle of it. Then I saw the blood.

What, then, shall we say in response to this? If God is for us, who can be against us? He who did not spare his own Son, but gave him up for us all—how will he not also, along with him, graciously give us all things? (Romans 8:31-32)

Since I can't fully explain what it's like to be the father of an only son, I know I can't describe seeing that only son's blood for the first time. I guess it's surprising that Caleb had lived a year without bleeding, but that didn't occur to me at the time. The sight of his blood overwhelmed me, and for a split second it paralyzed me.

Then I snatched him up into my arms. Quickly, and with furious gentleness I scanned his little body with my eyes and fingers to assess where he was hurt. Though the mirror had been scattered all around him, the only mark on his body was a small scratch on the inside of his left ear. Amazing—the inside of his ear! A trickle of blood flowed from it, but it was apparently more fear than injury that was bringing his tears. I guess that's what brought my tears too.

I can't read, hear, or even think of John 3:16 anymore without remembering Caleb lying in the middle of that broken mirror. That most familiar Bible verse had become trite to me, but now when I hear it I get a lump in my throat, thinking about what kind of determined, redemptive love could be strong enough to let an only son cry out in pain on a cross.

What kind of love lets an only son bleed?

Do you ever wonder if God loves you very much? Does it feel like he's your friend and generally on your side, but in a distant, general sort of way? Have you stopped recently to think of Jesus' death personally, as on your own behalf? Does contemplating God's great sacrificial love for you today make you want to tell him something?

You might also take a look at ... John 3:16; Romans 5:6-8

An Uninviting Birthday Party

Have you ever done something you didn't really have the authority to do? Did it turn out okay, or not?

When I was in first grade, I wanted to have a birthday party. A couple of my friends had just celebrated theirs, and giving a party seemed pretty easy. You just passed out the invitations, served and ate the cake, and collected the presents. My birthday was a whole three days away, and I figured that was plenty of time.

The next day during free time at school, I sat down and wrote out ten or fifteen invitations to my best friends. That's actually no small task for a first grader, and even though they were just on lined notebook paper torn into strips, I was pretty proud of my hand-made invitations.

At the end of the school day, I lingered in the classroom until everyone left, then went around and left the invitations inside my friends' desks. Then I went home and announced to my mom what I had done.

My poor mother had to deal with my presumptuous and inappropriate invitations. A lot of mothers would have just had a fit, then changed the plans they already had for that day, had three days full of stress, and pulled off some kind of a party. My mother sent me back to school to uninvite my friends.

For a long time I thought that was mean. Then I just figured she was too tired or too poor for the party. Then I thought she was just punishing me for not asking her first. As years passed and I looked back on that incident, I realized what a favor my mom did for me. Even at that early age, she helped teach me who had authority in our home and who didn't. Many of my friends began calling the shots in their homes at an early age, and their families are suffering for it even today.

> *Then the master told his servant, "Go out to the roads and country lanes and make them come in, so that my house will be full. I tell you, not one of those men who were invited will get a taste of my banquet."* (Luke 14:23-24)

There's a big difference in the "master" Jesus told about in this story and in my first-grade birthday invitations. The master had authority to invite whomever he wanted to his banquet. When his invited guests shunned his invitation and chose not to show up when the food was ready, he had the authority to reject them and invite brand-new guests, many of whom were "undeserving" strangers just passing through town.

God's authority can seem mean at times, or unreasonable, or even punishing. From my limited perspective, the things he chooses for me can feel unfair, or at least random. I'd much rather he just go with the flow of my plans and give his okay to what I've decided.

If he just gives me my way when I ignore or try to override his authority in my life, though, I'll soon be in deeper humiliation than I was with my first-grade friends. My mom did for me back then what God still does for me on a regular basis today— he reminds me that I'm here to fit into his plans more than he's here to fit into mine.

The nice part is that yielding to God's authority often transforms my plans into something infinitely better. That's how it worked with my mom, too. The next year I had a huge, really neat birthday party, and Mom even asked me to help write the invitations.

Who plans your parties?

How does God's authority present itself in your life? Is it more like a parent, a policeman, your best friend, or a brick wall you didn't see until you ran into it? How would you like it to be?

You might also take a look at . . . Matthew 7:28-29; Acts 5:27-29

Christ's return is sort of like ...

An Unexpected Crash

Does it ever bother you that Christ hasn't returned yet, even though Christians have thought he'd be back "soon" for almost 2000 years?

I almost died once. It was a rainy April day, and I was driving in the left lane of a busy four-lane road. At the intersection ahead of me, I could see a pick-up truck in the oncoming left lane, waiting to turn across my lane of traffic. I was sure he'd wait until after I got through the intersection. There wasn't nearly enough room between the car in front of me and my car for him to make it. Then, right in front of me, he started turning into my path, and his wheels began to spin. I was sure we would collide at about fifty miles per hour.

I've heard that in situations like that a few seconds can seem like a few minutes. Time seems to slow down as the panic of the moment sets in and adrenalin rushes into your system. It's true. It seemed I had a lot of time to think in the next ten seconds.

I wondered if I'd be killed or just badly hurt. I wondered who would call my family to come to the hospital. I wondered if my car would be totaled. I wondered how late I'd be for work, if I lived.

I'm still amazed at what happened next. As I pumped my

brakes and went into a skid, I veered around the truck to the left, crossing the two lanes of oncoming traffic. Miraculously for this time of day on such a busy street, there were no cars beside or behind the truck that had turned. As I fought the steering wheel back to the right, I crossed all four lanes of traffic on the slippery pavement. By then I had slowed down enough to think, I may get out of this without a collision! Then my car's right rear end swung around and banged into the guard rail, causing over a thousand dollars damage to my car. I then watched in my rearview mirror as the careless driver who had almost killed me drove his truck away. If I had died, I'm not sure he would even have known.

Now brothers, about times and dates we do not need to write to you, for you know very well that the day of the Lord will come like a thief in the night. While people are saying, "Peace and safety," destruction will come on them suddenly, as labor pains on a pregnant woman, and they will not escape. (1 Thessalonians 5:1-3)

Whenever the Bible talks about Jesus' return, it makes it clear that it will be sudden. There will not be time for last-minute preparation. Only ongoing, lifelong preparation will have value.

The suddenness of Jesus' return is true even for Christians today. It used to bother me that almost 2000 years have passed since Jesus said he would return "quickly." It helped me somewhat to understand that the word translated "quickly" or "soon" could also mean "suddenly" or "imminently." Still, it didn't seem right to me that generation after generation of Christians have lived expecting Jesus to return, and yet none of them have seen it happen.

My near collision with that truck made me see Jesus' return differently, however. I realized that, for me, dying in that car crash would have been Jesus' return. I also realized that generation after generation of Christians have stepped "suddenly" into death, and that for them time and history have ended and eternity has begun.

I'm not sure whether Jesus will come in the clouds during my lifetime, and I haven't stopped expecting him that way. But I have broadened my view of what it means to expect to be in his presence "suddenly," ever since that day it almost happened to me.

Could your crash come today?

Have you been thinking of Jesus' return in very general, far-off terms? Does the fact that he's delayed his return so long make you expect him in your lifetime or not? How does it affect your expectancy of Jesus' return today to realize its "suddenness" could be your death as well as his cloud-walking?

You might also take a look at . . . Matthew 24:27-31; 1 Thessalonians 4:13-18

DAY 34

Christ's return is sort of like . . .

A Class Reunion

Have you ever resented going somewhere simply because you weren't ready when it came time to go?

One of the things that takes the sting out of post-graduation good-byes is the promise of a reunion. Junior high, high school, college—all place you together with a unique group of people for a unique period of time in your life. Reunions promise you a trip back to when times and friendships were purer and simpler.

That's what they promise, anyway. I've only been to two reunions—one at my wife's school and one at my own school—but I think that will be enough for my lifetime.

At my wife's reunion, I didn't know anyone. She was bouncing around from person to person, catching up on old times and dutifully trying to introduce me and draw me into the conversation.

It seemed to me I had nothing in common with any of the people there and would probably never see ninety-nine percent of them again in my life. It was three of the longest hours I've ever endured.

You'd think my own reunion would have been better, but it wasn't. Oh sure, I got to reverse roles with my wife and bounce from person to person. Yet I wasn't having fun. Most of the handful of people I was closest to while in school weren't there for one reason or another. A lot of the people that were there seemed pretentious and preoccupied with showing off and comparing levels of success. On top of that, I didn't remember or recognize a lot of people. Inevitably it was the ones I didn't recognize that came up and called me by name. We left after about an hour.

> *For the grace of God that brings salvation has appeared to all men. It teaches us to say "No" to ungodliness and worldly passions, and to live self-controlled, upright and godly lives in this present age, while we wait for the blessed hope—the glorious appearing of our great God and Savior, Jesus Christ, who gave himself for us to redeem us from all wickedness and to purify for himself a people that are his very own, eager to do what is good.* (Titus 2:11-14)

I can think of at least three reasons why those reunions weren't fun for me, and those reasons help me understand why some people might not be excited about Christ's return.

First, I didn't really know who I was looking for. Since years and miles had separated me from these people, the relationships had grown distant, and the people had grown different. I hadn't maintained personal knowledge of them, nor they of me. Why should we be excited to see one another?

Second, I didn't do anything to prepare for the reunion. I could have browsed my old yearbooks, made some phone calls, worked on the reunion committee. I could have restored some relationships ahead of time—I could still do that, if I thought I'd ever go to another reunion.

Third, I had no joy at the reunion. Joy is something that can survive in all kinds of circumstances because you have hope—the eager anticipation of good—that what's coming is better. Because I hadn't invested in the relationships that were "reuniting," nor prepared to restore those relationships, I had not been "hopefully" waiting for the reunion. Living in hope prepares you for joy. The reunion event for me was a bust when it could have been a blast.

In his second letter to Timothy, Paul describes Christians as "all who have longed for his appearing." My reunion let me see how frighteningly possible it is to make Jesus' return a bust rather than a blast by not having a relationship now that longs for his appearing.

Ready for the reunion?

Are you building a relationship with Jesus day by day that is getting you excited about his return? If time and distance have come between you, what would it take to rekindle the relationship you once had? Could you start today? Can eternity be really enjoyable if you're not excited about reuniting with Jesus himself?

You might also take a look at . . . Philippians 3:17-21; 2 Timothy 4:8

DAY 35

Sharing your faith is sort of like . . .

Building a Bomb Shelter

Which communicates your faith more clearly, your words or your lifestyle? What do you think the people who only see your lifestyle can tell about what you believe?

There's an unusual house in the town where I used to live. When I first noticed the house, it was because of the large stack of bricks piled in the yard beside it. The house was already made entirely of brick, so I assumed the owner was adding on a garage or something. I started watching each time I drove by, to see what he would build.

It soon became apparent that he was making his own house bigger rather than building any additional structures. As weeks, months, then years passed, more and more bricks appeared in his yard, and the house grew and grew. I began to notice that he was putting layers of some other material between the brick layers and that he wasn't really building additional rooms, just additional layers.

One day I was driving by with a friend, and pointed out the unusual cocooning house to him. My friend had read about the man's project in the local paper, and informed me that he wasn't adding rooms or living space at all. He was making his house into a huge bomb shelter in anticipation of eventual nuclear war.

I laughed out loud. What a waste! How many thousands of other things he could be doing with his time and money! Did he think the whole town would blow up and he'd be left safe and sound in his cocoon eating pork and beans out of a tin plate?

My friend, however, didn't find his eccentricity as ridiculous. His philosophical statement made me think.

"I guess different people buy their life security in different ways," he said.

See how the siege ramps are built up to take the city. Because of the sword, famine and plague, the city will be handed over to the Babylonians who are attacking it. What you said has happened, as you now see. And though the city will be handed over to the Babylonians, you, O Sovereign Lord, say to me, "Buy the field with silver and have the transaction witnessed." (Jeremiah 32:24-25)

I'm intrigued with the man who was (and probably still is) building his house into a giant bomb shelter. I'd like to see the inside of that house. I'd like to sit and talk with him. I'd like to hear what he thinks about his investment now that the iron curtain is down and the Soviet Union has dismantled. I wonder if he feels foolish, or if he'd just say, "You wait and see."

I'm even more intrigued with what Jeremiah did. God had told him that the country was going to be overrun, the holy capital of Jerusalem taken, and the people whisked off into exile in Babylon. Then he told him to go buy some land.

What a great sense of humor God has! If there was ever a time when Judean real estate values were low, it was when the Babylonians were about to take over and export God's people to Babylon as slaves. But God wanted his prophet to publicly communicate a message of hope in the midst of his message of destruction and judgment. He wanted Jeremiah's lifestyle and actions to back up his words.

The man in the many-layered brick house is communicating a lot about what he believes by his actions, and it's clear that he believes doom will prevail even amidst many signs of hope. Jeremiah communicated just the opposite. It makes me want to do things in my lifestyle that are more like buying land than insulating myself in brick.

Are you buying land or building a bomb shelter?

If you could choose one public demonstration that would show people around you how you feel about life in Christ, what would it be? Where would you do it? How much would it cost, not just in time or money but in reputation? Would it be a big thing or a subtle, small thing? Could you do it today?

You might also take a look at ... Romans 1:16-17; 1 Corinthians 15:12-19

Creative Bible study is sort of like . . .

An Old Story Told a New Way

Are there times when the Bible seems to come more alive to you than others? When and why does that happen?

It was about twelve days before Christmas, and I found myself in charge of my youth group's Christmas party for about the fifth consecutive year. They were a fairly demanding group, always expecting something fun, creative, and new. I felt as though I had used my last creative Christmas idea the year before.

I turned to the familiar Christmas passage in the second chapter of Luke and began reading, hoping something would leap off the page at me. All that seemed to hit me was the same old stuff—shepherds, a stable, a manger, swaddling clothes, a Baby.

I felt like there was rich meaning in that great story of God's birth into the world, but how could we look at it in a fresh new way? Was there anything new to say about this familiar account that hadn't been said a million times before? Besides, my youth group was interested in things like fashion, science fiction, television, boyfriends and girlfriends. I kept reading the story, over and over. Then it hit me.

When it came time for the program at our youth group Christmas party, I divided the group into four or five groups and gave them a copy of the Luke account of Jesus' birth. I gave each group a box of props I had gathered. Then I asked each group to study the account and be ready in twenty minutes to act out the Christmas story as if it had happened in another setting—a futuristic space-age setting, the days of the Old West, a current-day boyfriend/girlfriend relationship.

They protested a little at first, but you should have seen the creative skits they produced in twenty minutes! They were allowed to change the setting, but knew they had to be accurate with the essential truth of the story. That meant they had to strip the story of incidentals, like sheep and stables, and focus on what was really important about God's incarnation.

There were guns, outrageous costumes, and unusual and irreverent baby deliveries. But it was God's word applied to a current setting in a way that made his truth come alive. It was creative Bible study.

> *When they had seen him, they spread the word concerning what had been told them about this child, and all who heard it were amazed at what the shepherds said to them. But Mary treasured up all these things and pondered them in her heart.* (Luke 2:17-19)

There's something about pondering God's Word while thinking about your current circumstances that inspires creativity. That's what Mary was doing, I think, when Luke said she treasured and pondered the "Word" that had been given her and the unusual way he came into the world. The shepherds ran off telling everyone what had happened. Mary pondered.

When you ponder something, you go beyond the obvious and superficial. Why shepherds? Why a virgin? Why physical birth instead of a magical appearance?

As my youth group labored to put together their skits, they had to grapple with questions like these. They had to know what they could change to fit their funny skits and what was sacred, eternal truth about the Christmas event.

To look at truth in a new way, to make it clearer without changing its essence is the measure of true creativity. For our group, true creativity began with pondering the truth rather than taking it for granted.

Pondered any old stories lately?

Does your personal Bible study ever lack something, like maybe your interest? Might pondering a familiar passage and trying to understand it in a new way open up some creative energy? What familiar passage could you approach creatively today?

You might also take a look at . . . Mark 4:30-34; Luke 2:1-20

DAY 37

Commitment is sort of like . . .

Flossing Your Teeth

Is commitment something that comes easily for you? How long does a commitment have to be before it's a real commitment?

I like my dentist. I don't like his assistant. It's nothing personal, and it's not that I don't like dental assistants in general. In fact, I liked his former dental assistant. She never nagged me about flossing.

The new dental assistant, on the other hand, is on a mission. She wants clean teeth in every patient and will stop at nothing in her zeal to accomplish that goal. The first time she cleaned my teeth, my whole mouth felt like a war zone. My gums were sore and bleeding a little. My jaw ached. My tongue tasted like stainless steel.

As I sat there recovering from the toughest cleaning I'd ever had, she started in on the flossing speech. Now, I hate to floss. I have pretty big hands, and a relatively small mouth, at least by comparison. To get that little string and my big fingers into the right cracks and crevices in my mouth isn't easy. I told her I'd try, then forgot about it.

Six months later, there I was in the war zone again, tasting the blood and experiencing the soreness. Then came the question: "How is the flossing going?"

I considered missing the rinse basin and splattering her white smock with whatever debris she had dislodged in my mouth, but I controlled myself and told a half-truth: "Well, not as well as I had hoped, you see I have these big hands...."

She listened with less than sympathetic patience, and asked me if I would try to do better so the cleaning wouldn't be as difficult. I grumbled that I would, and began working on my plan to deceive her.

A couple of weeks before my next appointment, I got out the dental floss and gave my teeth the old once over. About every other day until I saw the Delilah of Dental Doom, I flossed almost as well as I could. She didn't buy it. She told me I'd have to start coming back every four months instead of every six months so she could help me keep them clean.

> *The Lord has driven out before you great and powerful nations; to this day no one has been able to withstand you. One of you routs a thousand, because the Lord your God fights for you, just as he promised. So be very careful to love the Lord your God.*
>
> *But if you turn away and ally yourselves with the survivors of these nations that remain among you and if you intermarry with them and associate with them, then you may be sure that the Lord your God will no longer drive out these nations before you. Instead, they will become snares and traps for you, whips on your backs and thorns in your eyes, until you perish from this good land, which the Lord your God has given you.*
> (Joshua 23:9-13)

As the days of Joshua's leadership drew to a close, he called the people together and asked them for a commitment. It was a commitment that would cost them, but it was a commitment from which they would benefit greatly. They had only themselves to hurt by not following through on it.

Although I saw my dentist's assistant as my adversary and her demands on me as an infringement on my freedom, in reality the commitment she asked from me was for my own good. Eventually she got to me, not by explaining one more time how tooth decay works, but by giving me the consequences of my flossing disobedience. Either my commitment would be genuine, or I'd be hers to torture every four months for the rest of my life.

I could have terminated my relationship with that dentist, and perhaps found one whose assistant had lower standards. But my teeth and eventually my health would have suffered as a result. Commitment to God and his rules is much the same. He gives us tangible, real consequences to sloughing off on our commitment to him, in case we're not far-sighted enough to see the danger of disobedience to our spiritual health. Commitment, someone has said, is simply a decision spread over time.

What is spiritual flossing?

Does God's Word demand commitments from you that you don't consistently maintain? Have you agreed within yourself that those commitments are right, but put off getting disciplined about them? Have you noticed any consequences? Is there a discipline you need to commit to today?

You might also take a look at . . . 2 Kings 18:11-12; Matthew 7:21-23

Commitment is sort of like . . .

Stepping in Front of Your Dad

Do you choose to believe or commit to certain things mainly because your parents have? Is that good or bad?

As I walked to the president's office at my college, my mind flashed back to the one time I had been summoned to the principal's office in grade school. I wondered if I had done something wrong, or worse yet if he wanted me to do something I didn't want to do, like join the campus beautification committee.

That's probably why my mouth dropped open when he asked me to be the commencement speaker for my graduating class, along with my dad. I remember feeling surprised, then flattered, then fearful, then curious. Why us? Last year's speaker had been a famous personality, probably the most famous in our college's history.

As graciously as the president could, he helped me understand his choice. He didn't have much hope of "topping" last year's speaker, so he wanted to do something entirely and dramatically different. Instead of celebrity appeal, he wanted more of a grassroots approach—a student and his dad talking about their relationship. In the back of my mind I remember thinking, "Sure, then whoever you get the next year will seem famous by comparison."

Still, Dad and I undertook the project. We spent hours talking about our relationship—what it had been like to be my father, and what it had been like to be his son. I'll always cherish those hours we had together.

Once we had the content down, we faced the dilemma of how

two people could deliver an address like this. We finally agreed to do it in stages. From a podium at one end of the platform, he'd speak first on fathering a small child, and I'd respond perched on a children's chair at the other end of the platform. Then he'd describe fathering a grade school boy, and I'd give my perspective, having moved over to a school desk. He'd comment on fathering a teenager, and I'd move to a stool, my back turned to him and my arms crossed to demonstrate how closed I was to his leadership during that time in my life.

While he stayed at the podium throughout the address, I'd move slowly toward the podium, from children's chair to desk to stool. But how would we bring it to a close? How could we symbolize my maturity into my own beliefs and character? Then we agreed. He'd bow his head and step back from the podium, and I would take his place there for our closing remarks.

But if serving the Lord seems undesirable to you, then choose for yourselves this day whom you will serve, whether the gods your forefathers served beyond the River, or the gods of the Amorites, in whose land you are living. But as for me and my household, we will serve the Lord. (Joshua 24:15)

Most of us come to a point in our spiritual lives when we have to choose whether or not we'll take full ownership of the faith that's been taught us by others. That's not to say we don't have a faith of our own until then, but there's a sense in which we're "guarded" and kept accountable by those who have spiritually taught, nurtured, and discipled us. When they step back, we choose whether or not to step up to the podium we've seen them occupy.

Joshua gave the Israelite people that choice before he stepped out of leadership, having brought them into the promised land and led them in conquest of the peoples there. He reminded them that they had forefathers who served other gods and that they would live among people who still did so. Then, with one last reminder of where he stood, Joshua stepped back and left open a choice that we all make at some time in our spiritual journeys.

Have you stepped to the podium?

To what extent do you feel you "own" your beliefs and spiritual commitment? If you were separated from the spiritual leadership of your parents or other "leading" Christians in your life, are there some things you might abandon? What would they be? A lot of people come to this point when they go off to school or move out of their parents' house for the first time; what choices come with that point in life that are critical spiritual decisions?

You might also take a look at . . . 2 Kings 2:1-14; John 14:11-12

Understanding Jesus' death is sort of like . . .

An Unexpected Checkmate

Do you think the forces of evil were surprised by Jesus' death on the cross? Have you ever realized that Jesus wasn't surprised at all?

My friend and I were walking outside the restaurant where we had just finished lunch, and happened upon a giant chess set in the lawn. Since we had a few minutes to spare, we decided to play a quick match. We knew it would be quick, because neither of us had played in years.

Probably at least half of the people who learn to play chess also learn one or two "fool's moves." These are a series of four or five moves that can lead quickly to checkmate if your opponent doesn't realize what you're doing and move to defend his or her king. If your opponent does know what you're doing (or is even a moderate chess player), the fool's move is fairly easy to stop.

The success of the fool's move depends on your opponent being more preoccupied with setting up her or his strategy than defending against or even recognizing yours. The early moves of a chess game are often routine, even predictable. Checkmate never comes that early. Unless, of course, you're a fool and don't see it coming.

Hoping that my friend was as rusty as he confessed to be, I decided to drag the fool's move out of my memory and try it on him. I made the first move, the second, the third, and fourth. Then my friend unexpectedly captured my queen. A few moves later he checkmated my king.

> *The reason my Father loves me is that I lay down my life—only to take it up again. No one takes it from me, but I lay it down of my own accord. I have authority to lay it down and authority to take it up again. This command I received from my Father.* (John 10:17-18)

Expert chess players don't usually get checkmated by surprise. In fact, the great chess masters will often lay down their king in admission of defeat many, many moves before checkmate is achieved. Novice chess players like me go for the quick, easy, obvious attacks, and only defeat opponents who play the same way. We like fool's moves.

Satan is the ultimate fool. In the Bible, a fool is not someone short on intellect, but someone short on fear of God. It's not that he can't reason, but that he reasons wrongly. He thinks he can disregard God's eternal principles. He thinks he can outmaneuver God's plan.

My favorite line from the Jesus Christ Superstar rock opera is the exchange between Jesus and Pilate. Pilate, Satan's puppet, says, "Why do you not speak when I hold your life in my hands? Why do you stay quiet? I don't believe you understand!"

Jesus' reply says it all: "You have nothing in your hands. Any power you have comes to you from far beyond. Everything is fixed, and you can't change it."

Checkmate.

Have you seen the chess master play?

What difference does it make to your faith to realize Jesus' life wasn't taken from him against his will? Do you face events even today that seem beyond control, or will you face "fools" who still don't believe he pulled off what he claimed? Can your spiritual eyes of faith discern what he might be doing behind the scenes in those situations to pull off a surprise checkmate?

You might also take a look at . . . Ephesians 3:8-12; Colossians 2:13-15

Healthy dating is sort of like . . .

Fishing, Not Hunting

How do you go about finding the right person to date? Does it ever feel like you'll never find someone special?

In my youth group there were two sets of twin girls, all the same age. All four were lovely, bright, intelligent young ladies with a lot going for them. More than just being in my youth group, they were my buddies, "my little sisters."

I remember one Bible study during their freshman or sophomore year when they and I were the only ones present. The study was on relationships, and specifically on dating. Before long into the discussion, the self-pity started emerging.

"There are no good guys who are Christians," one lamented.

"Yeah, and even if there were, they wouldn't ask me out!" another pouted.

From there the pity party just got worse. They were all going to be old maids. They could never pull off the steps it would take to hunt down and win a good guy these days. And if you demanded that the guy you date be a Christian, the odds just seemed to go from improbable to impossible.

I interrupted the depressing discussion and suggested we talk about hunting and fishing. Their disbelieving look made me realize I had just been labeled a "typical guy." I convinced them, however, that knowing the difference between hunting and fishing was the only way they'd learn to be content while waiting out the dating game.

Like a lily among thorns is my darling among the maidens. Like an apple tree among the trees of the forest is my lover among the young men. I delight to sit in his shade, and his fruit is sweet to my taste. He has taken me to the banquet hall, and his banner over me is love. Strengthen me with raisins, refresh me with apples, for I am faint with love. His left arm is under my head, and his right arm embraces me. Daughters of Jerusalem, I charge you by the gazelles and by the does of the field: Do not arouse or awaken love until it so desires. (Song of Songs 2:2-7)

Read through the lovely poetry of the Bible's Song of Songs and see how the girl appeals to her guy. She "attracts" him rather than stalking him. He notices her as a lily among thorns. He asks the "daughters of Jerusalem" to wait for love rather than force it ahead of its time.

The difference between hunting and fishing is noteworthy. In hunting, you know exactly what you're shooting for. You take the right caliber of weapon. You stalk your prey carefully. You use deadly force to bring it down.

Fishing is different. You know generally what you'd like to catch, but it could end up being a catfish, bluegill, or largemouth bass. You have some equipment, but the key ingredient is your bait. What will you choose to attract that unknown friend beneath the water? Will you try the spot by the log or the one in the middle of the lake? Once the bait attracts the fish, will you land it easily or have to "play it" a while? Once you've landed it, will you keep it or throw it back unharmed?

My twin friends were getting discouraged because they had been hunting, setting their sights on someone from a distance and becoming disillusioned when he wasn't all they wanted him to be. I asked them to consider becoming all God wanted them to be, and see what that bait attracted.

A hunter shoots from a great distance and hopes he likes what he finds when he approaches his felled prey. A fisherman relaxes, enjoys being out on the lake, and chooses his bait carefully. The fisherman knows whatever fish takes the bait has chosen him as much as he has chosen the fish. And he can always throw his catches back unharmed until he gets a keeper.

Ready to take up fishing?

Have you ever "set your sights" on someone before you knew anything much about them? Has just being yourself ever attracted someone special? Which process seems to have better results? Whether you're involved in these processes or not, why not look today and see how the relationships around you support "hunting" or "fishing."

You might also take a look at... Ruth 2:1-4:12; Proverbs 7:6-27

Sweet Tarts, M&Ms, and Hostess Cupcakes

Have the marriages you've observed made you look forward to getting married or made you nervous about it?

I didn't care much for weddings years ago. They seemed to me to be full of stiff clothes, rigid ceremony, and uptight people. Weddings are supposed to be the big day for both bride and groom, but in so many of the weddings I had attended, neither half of the couple seemed to be having much fun.

That must be part of where I got my less-than-ideal image of marriage in general. Dating sounded like fun. Sex sounded like fun. Even building a home together sounded like fun. Why didn't getting married sound like fun?

Fortunately, by the time my wife and I got married, we had decided that we wanted our wedding to be as fun and personalized as we hoped our marriage would be. We didn't want to have our ceremony, or our relationship, totally prescribed by tradition.

Your wedding day, hopefully, is a once-in-a-lifetime experience. It can set the tone for your new life together, and illustrate to others the unique tastes, dreams, and life commitments you hope to undertake. We wanted it to be in a place we treasured, with people we loved and respected, doing things that we genuinely enjoyed.

My wife doesn't care much for nuts, so we had Sweet Tarts candy instead. I don't like those fancy mints you always get at weddings, so we had M&Ms for me. And although my wife insisted on a fairly traditional wedding cake, my "groom's cake" was my favorite—a tower of individually wrapped Hostess Cupcakes.

Jesus answered, "How can the guests of the bridegroom fast while he is with them? They cannot, so long as they have him with them. But the time will come when the bridegroom will be taken from them, and on that day they will fast.

"No one sews a patch of unshrunk cloth on a old garment. If he does, the new piece will pull away from the old, making the tear worse. And no one pours new wine into old wineskins. If he does, the wine will burst the skins, and both the wine and the wineskins will be ruined. No, he pours new wine into new wineskins. "(Mark 2:19-22)

Jesus spoke of his relationship with his disciples in terms of a wedding celebration. The religious leaders around him wanted Jesus to live a somber, traditionally religious lifestyle. They wanted him to be pious, serious, legalistic, and conformable. They wanted him to be like them.

Jesus insisted, however, that he hadn't come to "fit in" to the old traditions of a religion that had lost touch with its God. He had come to start a new kind of relationship with fallen mankind, one based on faith rather than works, on love rather than regulations. No longer would the bride and groom be slaves of the wedding ceremony merely for the sake of tradition. The ceremony would now celebrate the personal, joyful union of the bride and groom. Jesus had no more place in the Pharisees' stuffy religion than new wine had in old wineskins.

Initially, my wife and I drew a few frowns and puzzled looks over the way we chose to do our wedding ceremony and reception. We also noticed that afterwards people didn't use the traditional wedding adjectives of "beautiful" or "formal" to describe the event. The adjective we heard almost unanimously was that our wedding was a lot of "fun." That's the way we wanted the wedding to be, and that's the way we want our marriage to stay. Weddings and marriages should be genuine fun and celebration because they reflect Jesus' relationship with his own bride, you and me.

Want a cupcake?

Which of the marriages around you today have given you the most positive view of being married? Which have given you less than positive views? Are you in the process of building relationships based on who you and the other person are as individuals rather than on the expectations of tradition? Are your relationships genuine and growing, or are you stuck in friendships and relationships that are defined by rules that others make up?

You might also take a look at . . . Genesis 2:18-24; Isaiah 54:5

DAY 42

**The power of words
is sort of like . . .**

Poison in the School Cafeteria

Of all the words you'll say today, what percentage will be positive or encouraging? What percentage will be negative or critical?

I stood in the lunch line at school, feeling self-conscious and very alone. It was the first day of classes, and I didn't know anybody. I had just transferred to this school, and most of the people my age already had their friends and groups established.

During the class I had right before lunch, I had answered a couple of questions aloud and even managed to say something clever in the process. I had felt the approving smiles of a few strangers, and wondered if any of them would eventually become friends. I wished desperately for a friend right then, so I wouldn't have to stand there alone in the lunch line.

Then, ahead of me in the cafeteria line, I noticed a girl who had just been in class with me. If I wasn't mistaken, she was one of the ones who had smiled at me. Eventually she turned her head enough for our eyes to meet, and I could see she recognized me.

We introduced ourselves, and small-talked for a couple of minutes about my being new and about the class. I was a little surprised at how direct and unguarded she was, but felt grateful for the new acquaintance. I was just feeling like we might get to know each other better when she said, "You know, you'd be kind of cute if your nose wasn't so big."

She said it playfully, almost as if she just wanted to see my re-action. I'm sure I blushed and tried to cover my embarrassment with some quick quip. All I really remember was getting out of the conversation as fast as I could. We didn't eat lunch together.

All kinds of animals, birds, reptiles and creatures of the sea are being tamed and have been tamed by man, but no man can tame the tongue. It is a restless evil, full of deadly poison.

With the tongue we praise our Lord and Father, and with it we curse men, who have been made in God's likeness. Out of the same mouth come praise and cursing. My brothers, this should not be. (James 3:7-10)

That girl in the cafeteria line had an opportunity to do powerful good with a small dose of kind words. Instead she chose to do great damage with a different dose—one that settled in my stomach like poison.

My impression is that she didn't think much about which kind of words she was serving up to the new guy behind her. I later found out she was a Christian, and I'm sure if she read this now she'd be embarrassed, and regret not having spoken differently. The Bible says that's exactly how the tongue works, and why it's so dangerous. It's not the carefully chosen words for God that go wild and cause such damage. It's the careless or flippant words we toss out to each other that curse and destroy. We can kid ourselves into thinking we've got our words under control. We can treat words like they're cute little leashed poodles that sometimes make a mess in the wrong spot but are basically tame and submissive. Instead the Bible says we're walking wild tigers, which by their very nature stalk people to tear them up. I can vouch for that. Just call me clawed.

Dishing out any poison?

What were the most hurtful things that were said to you this past week? Did the people saying them know how hurtful they were being? Have you ever noticed, perhaps too late, that something you said hurt someone deeply? Is it too late today to serve up to the person you hurt an antidote for the poison?

You might also take a look at... Psalm 39:1; Proverbs 21:23

True devotion to God is sort of like...

Shooting around by Yourself

Is true devotion to God proven more in a crisis or in everyday discipline?

Ever since I was a young boy, I've loved playing basketball. The nearest backboard and rim I could find during my grade school days was about five blocks from our house. Almost every day and in all sorts of weather I would dribble my old playground ball up to that wooden backboard, netless rim, and gravel court. The backboard and rim have long since been torn down, but I have a sizable scar on my right knee that still reminds me of the gravel.

My greatest dream at that age was to be like Danny Maddis. Danny was a three-sport varsity letterman as a sophomore, and was already setting all kinds of high school athletic records during his junior year. As I would bounce my treadless rubber ball up to that rickety old basket, I'd imagine myself as him, and in my inner heart I determined to practice hard on this gravel court for as long as it took to be that good.

It was a spring day, and I had just released one of those "dream" shots when a voice from behind me interrupted my fantasy.

"How's it going?"

It was Danny. He was walking by my humble home court, had strolled up behind me just like a real person, and was holding his hands out asking me to throw him the ball. I did.

The next few minutes were utopia for me. It was just me and Danny, "shooting around." A few minutes later a car full of high school guys pulled over and emptied onto the court. Soon they had decided to play a pick-up game, and I walked over to the sideline where I had watched so many games when older guys took over the court.

"Hey, where are you going?" It was Danny's voice; I knew it by heart now. "You're going to be on my team." And I was.

> *Philip found Nathanael and told him, "We have found the one Moses wrote about in the Law, and about whom the prophets also wrote—Jesus of Nazareth, the son of Joseph."*
>
> *"Nazareth! Can anything good come from there?" Nathanael asked. "Come and see," said Philip.*
>
> *When Jesus saw Nathanael approaching, he said of him, "Here is a true Israelite in whom there is nothing false."*
>
> *"How do you know me?" Nathanael asked.*
>
> *Jesus answered, "I saw you while you were still under the fig tree before Philip called you."*
>
> *Then Nathanael declared, "Rabbi, you are the Son of God; you are the King of Israel."* (John 1:45-49)

Something happened under that fig tree that was just between Jesus and Nathanael. Since Jesus described Nathanael as a devoted Israelite, perhaps Nathanael was diligently praying there for Israel's Messiah to come soon. Maybe that fig tree was Nathanael's secret place to pour out his heart before God, to express his anticipation and longing for Israel's deliverance. Whatever happened under that fig tree, Jesus' knowledge of Nathanael's private moment there was enough to transform Nathanael's skepticism about Nazareth into passionate belief in Jesus.

Until I "shot around" with Danny that day, I had been an admirer, a humble fan whose hopes of being like Danny were tempered with skepticism that my rubber basketball could ever get me there. On the gravel basketball court that was my fig tree, I daily expressed my desire to live in Danny's world and my commitment to the disciplines I knew Danny would require. Then he came into my life and asked me to play on his team. Whatever devotion I had been expressing in my daily practice was overshadowed by his very presence. Nathanael, I understand.

Are you shooting around?

Does your daily devotion to God demonstrate the passionate discipline of wanting to live in his world and be like him? Where and how do you "shoot around?" Might being truly devoted to God require some changes in your daily routines and disciplines? Ready to start today?

You might also take a look at ... Ecclesiastes 12:13-14; Matthew 6:5-6

DAY 44

*Deliberate disobedience
is sort of like ...*

A Startle in the Magazine Section

Do you ever deliberately do things that are wrong, even realizing they're wrong as you're doing them? Should that be able to happen to a Christian?

Do you enjoy sneaking up on people and startling them? I do. I get a kick out of watching a suspenseful TV show with someone who really gets involved in it, then jumping at them with a screech at the most intense, dramatic moment. I also get slapped and hit a lot.

One of the best jumps I ever got out of anyone was one afternoon when two friends from my high school youth group and I were killing time in a shopping mall. We had gone our separate ways within one large department store, and agreed to meet later at the front of the store. I finished my browsing well before our meeting time, and decided to look around in the magazine section.

As I came around the corner, I saw my two friends peering into a certain magazine known for its "revealing" pictures. I overcame my shock and disappointment in them quickly enough to see an opportunity for a laugh.

Sneaking up quietly behind them, I mustered the deepest, sternest, fear-of-God voice I could. Slapping a big hand on each of their guilty shoulders, I thundered, "The rapture has come, and you've been caught with your nose in a pornographic magazine!"

Were they startled and embarrassed! We almost had to call for a cleanup in aisle twelve.

> *On the Lord's Day I was in the Spirit, and I heard behind me a loud voice like a trumpet... I turned around to see the voice that was speaking to me... When I saw him, I fell at his feet as though dead. Then he placed his right hand on me and said: "Do not be afraid. I am the First and the Last."*
> (Revelation 1:10, 12, 17)

John, the writer of this inspired passage, was perhaps Jesus' closest friend when he was on earth. Now, as an old man exiled on an island, John heard Jesus' voice, probably for the first time in sixty years. Though he knew Jesus intimately, the sight of the awesome risen Lord drove him to the ground as a dead man.

After years of faithful discipleship, Jesus' revelation of himself was still terrifying to John. No doubt he recognized the voice, but had no choice but to fall powerless in the presence of God the Son.

I'm confident that Jesus' return will be at least as sudden and awesome for me, whether I meet him in a hospital bed, in a car crash, or "in the air" at the end of time. More than once I've wondered exactly what I'll be doing when he comes for me. To my chagrin and disgrace, I've had that thought right in the middle of doing something I knew I shouldn't.

It makes me wonder how much I believe he's coming back like he said he would. If I really believed he might come right now, would I deliberately disobey him? Will I really risk having my own words come back to haunt me: "The rapture has come and you've been caught" ... doing what?

Startled humility seems to be the only way to meet Jesus at his return, and I'm certainly planning to be flat on my face, hopeful that he in his grace will beckon me to rise as he did with his old friend John. Maybe keeping that picture in my mind will help me stay clear of deliberate disobedience.

Ready to drop that magazine?

Putting aside those "oops sins" for a minute, are there times when you defiantly choose to do wrong? Can you visualize Christ returning during those moments? Does picturing that scene right now make you want to look for the nearest exit from whatever disobedience you may be choosing?

You might also take a look at ... Acts 5:1-11; 1 Corinthians 3:11-17

DAY 45

Real friendship is sort of like ...

Name Recognition

Do you think of God as a best friend? What does that mean to you?

It's not unusual for a close friendship to develop between people who see each other frequently. Many "best friends" are next-door neighbors, have lots of classes together, or share passions such as sports or music that bring them together often.

For some reason, my best friendships stopped following that pattern after junior high. I worked with one best friend, and then he moved to a job in another town. I made a best friend my first year of college, then I transferred to a different school. I roomed with another best friend in the college where I transferred, but now he lives hundreds of miles away.

There was also the best friend I met my freshman year in high school. We went to the same church, but that was really the only time our paths crossed naturally. He lived in a nearby town, went to a different high school, played different sports, had different hobbies. Yet we were in many ways closer than brothers. We could practically read one another's minds, and frequently finished one another's sentences.

Our telephone conversations always began the same way. My innocent "Hello?" would be greeted with a one word growl, usually barked at top volume like you'd expect from the football lineman he was:

"Adams?!"

"Scott!" I'd reply with as manly a growl as I could muster. (Scott was his last name—we were always too cool to use each other's first names except during rare moments of vulnerability). The conversation would go on from there to any of the many topics that formed the core of our relationship, but every conversation always began with the same tribal greeting.

We live hundreds of miles apart now, and our phone conversations are months apart rather than minutes. But to this day he could pick up the phone and bark "Adams?!" in my ear and I'd know to bark "Scott!" right back without a moment's hesitation. More importantly, our friendship would pick up instantly at the same deep level. That's not as good as him living next door, but it's close.

The man who enters by the gate is the shepherd of his sheep. The watchman opens the gate for him, and the sheep listen to his voice. He calls his own sheep by name and leads them out. When he has brought out all his own, he goes on ahead of them, and his sheep follow him because they know his voice. But they will never follow a stranger; in fact, they will run away from him because they do not recognize a stranger's voice. (John 10:2-5)

If you wanted to, you could find my phone number, call me and bark "Adams?!" in my ear right now. But I wouldn't answer "Scott!" because I'd know you weren't him. I know his voice. I know his intonations. I know his growl. I know him.

Jesus described himself as the Good Shepherd whose sheep recognize his voice because they are led by it every day. They genuinely listen to it, because they know their very lives depend on hearing it. They know the difference between the Shepherd and the stranger. They know the Shepherd is their true friend.

There is such a thing as a "friendship of convenience." Those kinds of "friends" don't really know each other. In fact, they're more like a stranger than a shepherd. They're "friends" only because they're in the same social group or because it's somehow mutually beneficial to hang around together. They may spend more time together than Scott and I ever did, but they don't recognize one-word phone greetings.

We all have casual friends, but I want to avoid having convenient friends that I might use rather than really know. Such relationships teach me bad habits about my friendship with my Shepherd. I need the kind of relationship—the kind of friendship—with God that lets me readily recognize his voice. I want to be able to move quickly and decisively when my Shepherd warns me of danger. I want to smile quickly and gratefully when he shows me love and faithfulness.

I think I may know one of the reasons God has placed my best friends across the country rather than across the street. Relying on a voice until you can see a friend face to face is pretty good practice for a friendship with God.

Recognize the voice?

If you categorized all your friendships as "best," "casual," or "convenient," how would they sort out? Which word best describes your relationship with God today? How do you turn a casual or convenient relationship into a genuine friendship? Does the same process apply to your friendship with God?

You might also take a look at . . . Proverbs 18:24; John 15:13-15

DAY 46

"Growing up" spiritually is sort of like . . .

Getting to Know Your Grandparents

How has your relationship to God changed since you first met him? Is God doing things differently, or are you?

One of my two grandfathers died when I was seven years old. The other grandfather is still alive today. I know them in entirely different ways.

To me, the grandfather who died when I was a boy was a

122

combination of Santa Claus and Mr. Fix-it. At the end of our two-hour drive to his and Grandma's house, my older brother and I inevitably had a "play purty" (as he called it) waiting for each of us. Just as inevitably, we'd break some part of that play purty during the first hour after we received it.

We never worried about it, though. Grandpa could fix anything without even getting up from his recliner. He'd merely reach into his pocket for his little pocket knife and—presto—it was as good as new, or better. My seven-year-old mind had little doubt that he could fix any toy, any car, any nuclear reactor with that magic pocket knife. Grandpa didn't have much, financially speaking, but when he died money was designated to buy my brother and I our first bicycles. The only way I really knew him was as a giver.

My other grandfather is equally as generous, and as children we always had special treats at his house, too. The difference is that Grandaddy is still alive, and I've come to know him as an adult, as I did both my grandmothers. I've talked to him about his life, his marriage, his career, his tough decisions, his faith. He's not Santa Claus and Mr. Fix-it, but he's one of the most inspiring men I've ever met.

> *Then they asked him, "What must we do to do the works God requires?"*
>
> *Jesus answered, "The work of God is this: to believe in the one he has sent."*
>
> *So they asked him, "What miraculous sign then will you give that we may see it and believe you? What will you do? Our forefathers ate the manna in the desert; as it is written: 'He gave them bread from heaven to eat.'"*
>
> *Jesus said to them, "I tell you the truth, it is not Moses who has given you the bread from heaven, but it is my Father who gives you the true bread from heaven. For the bread of God is he who comes down from heaven and gives life to the world."*
>
> (John 6:28-33)

A lot of the people who followed Jesus initially were preoccupied with his miracles. Why? Well, it seems those people were also preoccupied with their own needs and desires. Some were sick, and Jesus gave them health. Some were hungry, and Jesus gave them food. Some were powerless and poor, and Jesus gave them hope that the Messiah had come.

I used to look forward to seeing my Santa/Mr. Fix-it grandpa as much for what I knew he'd do for me as for who he was as a person. Today, I look forward to seeing my grandaddy because I long to know more of his character, his integrity, his wisdom. I want to be like him, and I cherish every moment we have together. It's not that he's changed in the past few years to make himself more attractive or desirable as a person. I just grew up, and maturity changed my perspective on him.

As I "grow up" in God's presence, I see the self-oriented immaturity in only approaching him for a play-purty. I still do it from time to time, but I wonder if he doesn't shake his head as I walk away to break it, patiently waiting for me to realize that the giver far outshines the gift. Jesus must have felt the same way when those around him valued perishable manna over the very bread of life who was in their presence.

I wish I could know my grandpa now, from a more grown-up perspective. I'm also very grateful to have known my grandaddy's character as an adult. It makes me want to abandon some of my "please give me" prayers for "who are you?" prayers.

Which kind of grandfather do you have?

Do you have a human relationship that seems to parallel your relationship with God? Is there another relationship that you'd rather model your devotion to God after? Why is that relationship a good one to apply to the way you seek God? What kinds of character-seeking questions could you pray right now to help you know him better?

You might also take a look at . . . Numbers 11:7-34; 1 Corinthians 13:11-12

*Starting a relationship the
right way is sort of like...*

The Wrong Boyfriend
and the Right Questions

*Have you ever had a relationship make it or not make it
depending on how that relationship started?*

From the moment I first met Beth, I wanted to know her better. She was (and still is) charming, smart, beautiful, and I had great plans for our relationship soon after our eyes met in a registration line at school. It took me only three or four conversations to ask her for a date.

Unfortunately, that's when I found out that she had a boyfriend. He lived in another town, but he was a boyfriend nonetheless. I was crestfallen. It didn't surprise me that someone that great was "taken," but I was heartbroken at the thought we wouldn't even have a chance together.

Then she gave me a glimmer of hope. We couldn't "date," she said, but we could still get to know each other better. That made me feel about as good as her saying we should be "just friends," the most dreaded concept in modern dating. I remember thinking that she was just being nice, and pretty much gave up on the idea that our relationship would ever go any further. Still, my heart hurt.

Then came that fateful Friday afternoon when everything changed. She was coming out of the cafeteria with her friends. I was going into the cafeteria by myself. We paused just outside the door to exchange hellos, then walked our separate ways to the sound of her friends' giggling. I remember shaking my head again with fresh disappointment that our relationship had been drenched before it could be kindled.

Moments later I turned around in the cafeteria line and saw her approaching, this time by herself. She asked if she could join me, and for the next half hour she got to sit and watch me eat spaghetti. Then we walked outside and sat down on a fairly remote bench. Somehow I felt the future of our relationship was on the line, and I wondered what I could possibly say to keep it alive.

... and find out what pleases the Lord. (Ephesians 5:10)

This short verse tells us to start and grow our relationship with God by finding out what pleases him and doing it. So many times we try to start a relationship by being impressive. We craft a strategy of looking a certain way, acting a certain role, and then having our best friends "scout out" what our chances are with the person who is our "objective." Even if it works, we've come closer to achieving a goal than we have to starting a human relationship.

Because Beth eventually became my wife, I tend to believe the question that came to my mind during that tense moment on the school bench was providentially inspired. As we sat down and looked at each other with that "now what?" look, I simply asked her to tell me about her favorite things. My desire to get to know her while I had this chance overshadowed my need to impress her. That desire to know her was so intense that I felt I had to find out what pleased her, what kinds of things she loved. Why? I had hopes of being on that list someday, and I thought she might give me some clues on how to get there.

For the next four hours, we exchanged favorite things. She talked about rainbows, her puppy, sunsets, evening walks, and her love-worn teddy bear. I talked about basketball, writing, music, and making people laugh. A few weeks later, I would sing a song to her that I had written about her favorite things. She told me that was a key moment in our relationship. Within a month the distant boyfriend was history.

Are you asking the right questions?

If you're in a dating relationship now, how did it start? Did the way it started help determine the way it's going now? If you're not in a dating relationship right now, do you "have your eye" on someone? Can you think of a way to get to know that person better that focuses on who he or she is and what pleases him or her? How might this relate to your relationship to God, even today?

You might also take a look at . . . Genesis 29:9-28; John 4:7-30

Serving is sort of like . . .

Being the Best Man Instead of an Usher

Does serving others come easy to you or do you have to work at it? Do you work at it?

I tend to be a spotlight type of person rather than a behind-the-scenes type of person. I enjoy being with people. That's why I'd rather be an usher than a best man in a wedding. Ushers get to meet everyone. They get to parade up and down the aisles—welcoming, smiling, escorting, helping, being charming.

So when my friend asked me to be the best man in his upcoming wedding, I had mixed feelings. I knew it was an honor to be asked. I knew there would be a lot of people there I'd enjoy seeing. I knew it would be fun. But I had been a best man once before, and I knew I had missed a lot of that good stuff by being the best man. Why? Because the best man's primary role is

to serve the bridegroom, to tend to his needs, to stand in his shadow.

I couldn't really picture that happening in this case. My friend was a soft-spoken, modest man marrying a quiet girl. That's not a very big shadow to stand in. I remember thinking that I'd much rather be an usher in this wedding.

Nevertheless, I agreed to be the best man. As unnatural as the role was for me, expressing love and service for my dear friend was the most natural thing in the world. I realized as I ran errands, straightened his tie, drove him around, and stayed in the background that I wouldn't do this for just anybody. Why, then, was I having so much fun doing it for him?

> *"You yourselves can testify that I said, 'I am not the Christ but am sent ahead of him.' The bride belongs to the bridegroom. The friend who attends the bridegroom waits and listens for him, and is full of joy when he hears the bridegroom's voice. That joy is mine, and it is now complete. He must become greater; I must become less."* (John 3:28-30)

Something spiritual happened to me on the wedding day of

my quiet friend. It took a deliberate act of my will to stay at his side, to make sure he had what he needed, to run his last-minute errands. In our past relationship, he had sometimes taken the backseat to my stronger, more outgoing personality. On that day, I determined ahead of time that my role was to point people to him, and to make it the happiest day of his life. As best man, my needs had to come second to his needs, and his needs changed my needs entirely.

That must be what John the Baptist meant when he said that his Lord (and his younger cousin), Jesus, must become more important while he became less important, less prominent. John strikes me as the kind of man who had never played second fiddle to anyone. He was a bold, rough, outspoken man—greater than all the prophets before him, Jesus said. Yet this strong, center-stage prophet recognized that when the bridegroom comes, the best man rejoices both in his presence and in his service.

Serving Christ, being his "best man," isn't something that comes naturally to me. It's not necessarily that I want to be the bridegroom, but sometimes I'd rather be part of his wedding as an usher—the way I want to do things—rather than in the serving, best man role to which I was invited. To do so, I have to take the driving needs and priorities of my life and deliberately de-emphasize their control over me. I have to let what's important to him have ever-increasing control. I have to make pointing to him and making him happy more important than parading down the aisles my way.

Would you rather be an usher?

Do you ever catch yourself wanting God to be your "best man" instead of your being his? Are you willing for him to be Lord even if he asks you to play a role that you don't enjoy? In what way today might you live out John the Baptist's statement, "He must become greater; I must become less?"

You might also take a look at... 1 Corinthians 15:9-10; Hebrews 3:1-6

The Newton Street Water Fountain

How would you describe the time when you came into right relationship with God? Was the dominant feeling joy? Relief? Humility? Freedom?

The best water in the world is from the water fountain at the Newton Street Ball Park in the small town where I grew up. Now I know that's a biased, subjective judgment on my part, and that almost anyone else could make a similar claim about the best water they've ever tasted.

I guess that's my point. Anyone who's asked to identify the "best water in the world" will probably admit they haven't tasted the entire world's water supply, yet they're also likely to call to mind the most refreshing drink of water they've ever personally experienced. Remembering that most refreshing drink is certainly a compliment to the water, but it's also a testimony to the severity of the thirst. Exceptional water can taste average when you're not thirsty. Average water can taste exceptional when your thirst is desperate.

That's why, for me, the best water ever was at Newton Street. There my childhood friends and I would play too hard and too long—sometimes all day—at our sandlot baseball marathons. We would sweat, slide, and soak up the dirt from the grassless infield. We'd inhale and ingest more of that dirt than you would think possible. I think it was there I first learned to spit for distance.

As the sweat and spit poured out, the sun and dirt poured on. Left alone, the human body only loses moisture, it can't manufacture it. As much as was possible in my limited boyhood experience, I grew very, very thirsty.

"Come, all you who are thirsty, come to the waters; and you who have no money, come, buy and eat!" (Isaiah 55:1)

The prophet Isaiah wrote both from a time and from a hot, arid place where genuine thirst was a daily reality and where dangerous thirst often threatened life itself. He used an image to communicate God's offer of saving mercy with which the people of his day could intimately identify.

No traveler on the dusty roads of Isaiah's day would have turned down the offer of a cool drink of life-giving water. For food to have been offered freely as well would have been unbelievable to them. The thirstier and hungrier the traveler, the more gratefully the offer would have been accepted.

I realize that I've never known real, dangerous, life-threatening thirst. But at my thirstiest moment, the Newton Street water fountain was my oasis of mercy. I had no resources to satisfy my own thirst, and that fountain refreshed me for my bike ride back to where my mom had the free food waiting. Recalling the cool refreshment of that water fountain gives me an image that parallels what Jesus did for me when he gave me the merciful, living water of salvation. And I guess it makes the water at Newton Street second best, after all.

Remember being thirsty?

Do you still have a sense of the desperate situation you were in before God rescued you? Could recalling the circumstances and sensations of your salvation experience help you live more faithfully today? Any idea why God made thirst a daily experience for us?

You might also take a look at . . . John 4:7-15; John 7:37-38

Hypocrisy is sort of like . . .

Being Both Nearsighted and Farsighted

Do you ever feel like you have two separate lives, one that's spiritual and one that's not?

I used to have 20/20 vision. But in the past couple of years my eyes have done a funny thing. My left eye has gradually gone farsighted, while my right eye has gradually gone nearsighted.

Oddly enough, I never really noticed the change. Apparently my eyes have worked out a coordination between them so that when I'm reading, my right eye does all the work, and when I look up for distances, my left eye kicks in and does all the work.

My surprising discovery of this phenomenon came when I had to take the vision test for my driver's license renewal, an every-four-years event where I live. When the clerk asked me to read what I saw in the little viewer, I only read half of the screen. My left eye, it seems, was on break.

She asked me to read the rest of the line. I looked back in the viewer and read the same abbreviated line. That wasn't good enough for her. As she spun the viewer around to make sure it was functioning correctly, I noticed that each eye was supposed to look down its own side of the viewer. As she spun it back around, I was able to read the left side—at least most of it—with my right eye. With twenty-seven people behind me in line, she decided that was close enough to pass.

Shortly afterwards, I visited an eye doctor for the first time and gave him a good chuckle as well. He prescribed some eye-glasses for me that helped each of my eyes see what the other had been enjoying rather exclusively. I rarely wear them, however. As long as the eyes are taking turns at the appropriate times, why should I?

> *And he said to them: "You have a fine way of setting aside the commands of God in order to observe your own traditions! For Moses said, 'Honor your father and mother,' and, 'Anyone who curses his father or mother must be put to death.' But you say that if a man says to his father or mother: 'Whatever help you might otherwise have received from me is Corban' (that is, a gift devoted to God), then you no longer let him do anything for his father or mother. Thus you nullify the word of God by your tradition that you have handed down. And you do many things like that."* (Mark 7:9-13)

Jesus said to the Pharisees that they couldn't just park their religion in the corner and call on it when it served their purposes. They shouldn't set aside "Corban" money, pretending it was for God, when in fact they just wanted to avoid their responsibility of caring for their parents. Hypocrites do things like that because their main agenda in life is their own will and priorities. Religion is something they use as a means to an end.

I don't want my living faith to behave like dead religion, yet too often I separate my "devoted" life from my "daily" life the same way my left and right eyes have separated their vision responsibilities. It's almost as if I have designated times when the devoted part of me is supposed to do all the work, make all the decisions, determine my thoughts and behavior. Other times I let the devoted part of me "take a break."

There shouldn't be a "devoted" versus "daily" schizophrenia in the Christian's life. The only way I know to keep it from happening is to let my devoted life govern my daily life. As long as I have a daily "regular life" agenda from which I want to keep my devotion to God separate, I have only a cheap devotion. It's a devotion that can see only so far, and isn't likely to pass God's vision test for driving my life safely under his care. In the words of an old hymn:

Be Thou my Vision, O Lord of my heart;
Nought be all else to me, save that Thou art.

How's your vision?

Are there subtle ways in which you've separated your life before God from your life before others and your own goals? How well are the two lives coordinating? In order for your devoted life to govern your daily life today, what kinds of decisions might you have to make right now?

You might also take a look at . . . Matthew 23:12-14; Luke 22:54-62

A destructive tongue is sort of like . . .

Nicknaming Boogers

Have you ever found out that something you said casually or flippantly had great impact on other people? Was it impact for their good or for their harm?

Do you have a nickname? Have you ever given anyone else a nickname? I remember a girl from my fourth grade class whose nickname was "Boogers." I didn't give her the nickname, but I have to admit I did my share to perpetuate it. We used to play "Boogers tag" on the school playground during recess. We pretended that it was hideous to have to stand by her in line. If she brushed up against us, we had a mock purification ritual to wash off the germs. We were pretty cruel little boys.

It didn't take Boogers long to pick up on the games we were

playing. Yet for some reason, it didn't seem to bother her. In fact, she began playing along with our cruelty, chasing us at recess and touching us in line or in the hallway to give us Boogers' germs. It was like she believed her nickname.

The only place I ever saw Boogers was at school—until the day she showed up at my church. I didn't know what to do. We'd been talking in church about inviting friends to come, and how important it was to make people feel welcome. I was a fairly young boy to have to figure this one out, but I was also a Christian.

There I was, caught between the couple of school friends that knew she was Boogers and my church friends and parents and other adults who were urging me to welcome her and share the love of God with her. There she was, standing right in front of me, being introduced just as if she were a regular person.

Before I knew it, she had been left in my care to show around the church. As our eyes met for probably the first time ever, I almost saw her as a real, feeling little girl. In that brief, tender moment she reached her hand out to mine, and as they touched, she softly said, "You have booger germs!"

Out of the same mouth come praise and cursing. My brothers, this should not be. (James 3:10)

The tongue has the power of life and death, and those who love it will eat its fruit. (Proverbs 18:21)

Throughout the Bible we find that both spoken "blessings" and spoken "cursings" can have enormous power. We know it's true by our own experience. How many times have we met someone scarred by words such as "you never do anything right," "how could you be so stupid," or even "you'll always be my little girl." Yet it's just as easy to recognize someone who has been consistently praised, loved, and accepted. They seem to carry that sense of blessing with them all the time.

I'd like to be able to say I passed my test with "Boogers" nobly, apologizing for the nickname and its accompanying cruelty, and telling her I didn't want to be like that anymore. Maybe

that's too much to expect of a fourth grade boy. But is it too much to expect of a Christian? And if I can pass my behavior off as the immaturity of a fourth grader, what's my excuse today for the times I speak curses instead of blessings upon the people around me? What's my excuse for talking negatively and destructively about people when I could either hold my tongue or speak something positive or encouraging about them?

I didn't pass the fourth grade test nobly, even at church. She soon became Boogers there too, at least for the few short weeks she attended. While I was a little more subtle and careful with my Boogers games at church, I never translated her undeserved cursing into a blessing.

I don't know how much long-term impact my nicknaming had on that poor little girl. Maybe it's even "guilted" me more that it actually hurt her. But for what it's worth, Debbie, I do know your real name. And I'm sorry.

What kinds of nicknames are you using?

Who are the people about whom you're most likely to speak cruelly? Are there any positive, constructive things to be said about them? How might it affect your relationship with them to start speaking blessings rather than cursings about them? How might it affect your relationship with God? Could you start today?

You might also take a look at . . . Matthew 12:36-37; James 3:3-12

*Unhealthy friendships
are sort of like . . .*

A Tug-of-War in Front of a Freight Train

Do you have a sense that some of your friendships are better for you than others? How can you tell the difference between healthy friendships and unhealthy friendships?

It was the summer after my eighth grade year, and Tim and I were going to hang out together for the first time. Specifically, we were going to "go downtown." In the small town where I spent my grade school and junior high years, "going downtown" was one of the summer's main (and only) evening activities. If you were in high school and had a car, you "cruised" downtown. If you were in junior high and didn't have a car, you walked downtown.

Up to that point Tim and I hadn't spent much time together. He lived on the other side of town, and usually socialized with a wealthier, faster-paced crowd than was my reputation. I was flattered that, for the first time, he wanted to hang out with me. I made sure I had plenty of money to take with me. Tim always had plenty of money, and even though I knew mine was more earned than given and his more given than earned, I wanted to be able to afford whatever his tastes demanded that night.

When we got downtown, we played pool and pinball at the local "teen town" place. I was impressed at how many older kids Tim knew, especially older girls. We agreed to meet some of them there later, and then hoofed it across the railroad tracks that bisected the town to go get some ice cream.

On the way back we heard a train whistle. Tim's eyes lit up. "Come on, let's go!" he shouted, and took off running.

I trailed him haltingly. The train seemed pretty close to me. As we approached the track, the gates were down and the train was in plain sight. Tim didn't stop. He flew across the tracks, and turned to face me. I could see the train's oncoming headlight only a few hundred feet away. In those moments when the train was rattling down the track, it was like an invisible tug-of-war was taking place between me and my new buddy. I decided to stay on my side of the track.

When the long freight train had passed, Tim was waiting for me with an impatient, disgusted look. He couldn't believe I hadn't followed him across. I had detained him for almost five minutes. Perhaps more significantly, it seemed I had failed a test for risk taking and fast living that really disappointed him.

The rest of the night he was sort of mad at me. It seemed to me he was angry at me for who I was. Soon I was angry at him for who he was. For some reason, Tim and I didn't hang out together after that.

That day Herod and Pilate became friends—before this they had been enemies. (Luke 23:12)

Herod and Pilate were drawn together as "friends" for the worst possible reason. They both wanted to get rid of Jesus. Their friendship was based entirely on mutual self-interest. They saw they could help one another reach their selfish goals. It was actually more of an alliance than a friendship. Prior to the day when they joined forces against Jesus, they had been enemies.

If I were honest, I'd have to say I didn't have much basis for true friendship with Tim. He knew people and had things that I thought I wanted in my life. I thought hanging out with him might help me get them. He probably wanted something from me too, though I never had a chance to find out what. We were working more toward an alliance than a friendship.

Tim hurt my feelings when he didn't wait patiently for me that night. From that moment on, it was like he knew he'd always have to wait for me, and I wasn't worth it. I knew he'd always be asking me to do things I wasn't sure were right, and I wasn't sure he was worth it. In retrospect, it seems God spared me that summer night from something more destructive than a freight train.

Ready to drop your end of the rope?

How would you describe your relationships with people "in your group" who aren't really your friends? How many of your friendships are more like "alliances"? Are you hanging around with people for what they may be able to do for you rather than for who they are as your friends? Do you see any danger ahead in those relationships?

You might also take a look at . . . Deuteronomy 13:6-9; Psalm 41:9

Peer pressure is sort of like . . .

Playing for the Crowd

Who are the people whose approval you value the most? Does approval from all those people sometimes pull you in different directions?

Between my freshman and senior years in high school, the reasons I enjoyed playing basketball gradually changed. Up through my freshman year, I simply loved the game. Whether I was indoors or outdoors, by myself or on a team, in a uniform or in my jeans, I simply enjoyed putting the ball through the hoop. Our freshman team played on Saturday mornings, and we never had that many fans. That was okay. We were having fun just playing.

By my senior year, however, I had been gradually introduced to the concept of playing for the crowd. Between two and three thousand people came to watch each of our varsity games. There was a big pep band. We had fancy warm-up suits. Our very entrance onto the court was through a huge paper hoop with our team mascot and colors carefully hand painted on it. Every game was show time.

He who lives by the crowd, however, usually dies by the crowd. Just before my senior year we lost several key players who either moved or were injured, and we ended up having a terrible losing season. Often we heard as many groans and boos as we did cheers.

During the closing moments of one game, I remember standing out near center court waiting for another player to shoot a free throw. As I stood there, someone from the upper rafters launched a paper airplane that soared high above the crowd and onto the court, deftly landing at my feet. We were losing the game, as usual, and my inner need for cheers hadn't been met. So I picked up the airplane, redirected it back toward the crowd, and let it fly.

I guess I didn't have the prevailing air currents I needed because the plane made it only to the edge of the bleachers before it made a 180 degree upward turn and landed back at my feet. The cackles and jeers started. Quickly I picked it up again and threw it back toward the crowd, this time with more fervor and energy.

Once again it changed directions and returned to the court, this time at the feet of one of my competitors. Now the jeers were accompanied with a few unkind remarks comparing my basketball skill to my airplane-throwing skill. With a smirk on his face, the opposing player picked up the airplane, crunched it into a paper wad, and threw it over his shoulder into the bleachers, about halfway up. The crowd cheered.

Am I now trying to win the approval of men, or of God? Or am I trying to please men? If I were still trying to please men, I would not be a servant of Christ. (Galatians 1:10)

It's so easy to let the approval of those around me become my main standard. In some ways, that's easier than being governed by God's Word and the voice of his Spirit as it moves within my own personality and integrity. When the crowd is my standard, I merely do more of what they applaud and less of what they jeer. With God's standards and the strength of his character within me, I sometimes do less of what they applaud and more of what they jeer.

Shortly after the crumpled paper airplane left the court, so did I. My coach said something terse about sitting down and trying to remember why I was on the court. I suspected he meant it had little to do with aviation. When I returned to the court, I had to shut out the wisecracks and sneers that welcomed me. I was determined to regain some of that freshman love for the game, and to rely on a different standard than the crowd, whom I had allowed to become too important.

Are you playing for the crowd?

Have any of the crowds you play for steered you into behavior or attitudes that aren't your own? Has your dependency on their applause distorted the first loves in your life that should mold and motivate your conduct? Do you need to "change frequencies" today, so you tune out the crowd and tune in the Holy Spirit?

You might also take a look at... Psalm 1:1-3; Matthew 6:1-6

Being rejected is sort of like...

Little League Tryouts

Have you ever been rejected? Does the rotten way rejection feels mean nothing good can come from it?

A s she dropped me off for Little League baseball practice that day, my mom asked me what time she needed to pick me up. Though I was only seven or eight years old, I was already getting a little embarrassed at being driven around by my mother, and I took great pride in telling her I wouldn't need a ride home that day. This was the day the final team was being named, and those of us who made the team would be going in the coach's big pickup truck to pick out hats and jerseys after practice.

Mom looked a little hesitant, but didn't say anything. It was about two miles from this ball field on the outskirts of town to our house, and she didn't like the idea of my possibly not having a way home. But I assured her it was taken care of, and she left.

At the end of practice, the coach summoned everyone into the dugout. He thanked us all for coming out, and said he was sorry everyone couldn't make the team that year. I looked around sympathetically to the handful of guys I thought probably wouldn't make it. Then, one by one, he called the names of the guys who made the team, and asked them to run out to the pitcher's mound. He didn't call my name.

It was a lonely, rejected little boy who walked the two miles home that day. Kicking rocks all the way and crying more than just a little, I thought about how little I'd see of my two best friends who had made the team. I thought about how I didn't really want to see them now anyway. I thought about what I would say to my parents when I got home. I thought about my baseball skills—or lack of them. But by the time I got home, I was thinking about playing basketball instead of baseball that summer.

As you come to him, the living stone—rejected by men but chosen by God and precious to him—you also, like living stones, are being built into a spiritual house to be a holy priesthood, offering spiritual sacrifices acceptable to God through Jesus Christ. (1 Peter 2:4-5)

As odd as it may sound, there's something holy about rejection. When I transform my rejection into victory, I've done something Christlike. When I refuse to accept defeat as final, but show my detractors a surprise ending, I've chosen to exercise authority in my circumstances just as Jesus exercised authority over death and the grave. God is in the business of taking that which has been rejected and making something infinitely greater from it.

That summer when I didn't make the Little League team, I turned my rejection from baseball into a new love for basketball. Later that love would bring me not only great enjoyment, but honors, a college scholarship, and some of my life's best friendships. It would have been difficult to convince me during that long walk home from Little League tryouts that this humbling rejection would work out for the best in the long run. But sometimes a long solitary walk is better than a ride in the wrong pickup truck.

What do you do when you don't make the team?

What kind of rejection have you been handed recently? Is there a way to turn your disappointment into an opportunity for redirection? Might there be something better in store for you after you escape from self-pity?

You might also take a look at . . . Isaiah 53:3-12; Mark 8:31

Explaining what you believe is sort of like ...

A Game of Duck Duck Goose

Have you ever been asked to explain about what you believe? Were you surprised with your own answer?

Our youth group spent a week one summer on a mission trip to help out a small church in Vermont. Besides painting the church and working around its property, we were going to lead backyard Bible clubs for children in some of the church members' homes.

Just before the club started one afternoon, my partner Debbie and I were discussing how we'd explain salvation to some of the younger children. We didn't really come to any conclusions before the game time started, so we went ahead and played Duck Duck Goose with them.

On the outside chance that you've never played or heard of Duck Duck Goose, let me explain. Duck Duck Goose is a game where the children sit in a circle while the one who is "It" walks around tapping each one on the head and saying "duck." At some point, the child who's "It" says "goose" instead of "duck." The child who's, uh, "goosed," has to get to her or his feet and chase the child who is "It" around the circle in a race to get to the goose's original spot. If the goose doesn't catch "It," the goose becomes "It". If the goose does catch "It," that child has to sit in the middle of the circle until some other child is caught. Got it?

Later in the club, after the game and the Bible story about Zacchaeus, one of the younger children asked, "What did Jesus mean when he said salvation had come to Zacchaeus' house?"

Debbie looked at me, and I looked at her.

> *But when they arrest you, do not worry about what to say or how to say it. At that time you will be given what to say, for it will not be you speaking, but the Spirit of your Father speaking through you.* (Matthew 10:19-20)

After only a brief pause, Debbie dove in to answer the child's question about salvation. She said that when Jesus brought salvation to Zacchaeus, it was sort of like taking his place in the middle of the Duck Duck Goose circle. Zacchaeus' wrong choices and bad behavior—his sin—had put him in a penalty circle that only Jesus could get him out of. Salvation at Zacchaeus' house simply meant Jesus had saved him from that penalty circle so he could start all over, playing God's way from now on.

As you'd expect from curious children, the kids at this club had a dozen follow-up questions. Many of those questions would have challenged a highly educated theologian. The only thing that amazed me more than the depth of the children's questions were the answers Debbie found in examples like the Duck Duck Goose game. Soon I was helping her answer questions, and we were surprising each other with what was coming out of our mouths. Our surprise, however, was overshadowed by the rush we felt as God provided answers to each question that was asked, in terms even a child could understand.

We could hardly wait to get back to the rest of the youth group and tell them how God had given us such a great opportunity to teach in such an unusual way. As we walked away from the club, I told Debbie I was anxious to see if she could pull off the same thing the next day. She smiled and said she was sure she could if God and I would just choose the right warm-up game again.

Ready to surprise yourself?

Would knowing how to explain your faith to a child help you know how to explain it to people your age? To those who don't know Christ, is salvation more likely to appear too simple or too complex? Would mastering two or three simple analogies strengthen your ability to share the gospel?

You might also take a look at . . . Luke 19:1-10; 1 Corinthians 2:1-4

*Living expectantly is
sort of like . . .*

Wanting to Kiss Carol

*What are you really looking forward to with great antici-
pation? Does your anticipation influence the way you
live each day?*

When I started dating Carol, I was somewhat in awe of her. She was one of the prettiest and classiest girls I knew, the star of school plays and choral singing groups. Carol had been dating another guy for several months, and when their breakup made her available, I waited only the minimum, appropriate "mourning" time before seeing if I had a chance with her.

She said yes to one date, and then another, and I began to be convinced that she liked me as much as I liked her. I wanted to take the relationship slowly, to be a perfect gentleman, to treat her like a princess. She had just come out of a long relationship, we didn't know each other very well, and I didn't want to blow it. At the same time, I desperately wanted to kiss her.

I wanted to kiss her, not only for the obvious hormonal reasons, but also because I viewed a kiss as a certain milestone in a relationship. When a girl lets you kiss her, I reasoned, she sends a signal on where she wants the relationship to go. Depending on how she kisses you, she may send a signal on how fast she wants the relationship to go. Depending on how often she kisses you... well, you get the point.

So I waited several dates as I plotted my puckering plan. At the end of about the fourth or fifth date, I put my ego on the line in the classiest way I could think of. As I walked her to the door of her house, I politely asked, "May I kiss you good-night?"

What a gentleman! What a prince! Right? Her reply made my puckerer gape in disbelief. She merely smiled and said, "No, I don't kiss boys."

Therefore the Lord himself will give you a sign: The virgin will be with child and will give birth to a son, and will call him Immanuel. (Isaiah 7:14)

Behold, I am coming soon! My reward is with me, and I will give to everyone according to what he has done. (Revelation 22:12)

Both Isaiah and then John (over 800 years later) were asked to anticipate Jesus' arrival. Neither would see it happen in their lifetime. But as you read their writings, you sense that both Isaiah and John lived expectantly. The coming of their Messiah was not a long-shot event that each day would have to beat enormous odds. They talked about it. They wrote about it. They longed for it. They knew it could happen today.

After Carol postponed my kiss, I was extremely puzzled. She apparently had not turned me away, she had turned my kiss away. She assured me how much she liked me. She told me she considered our relationship romantic rather than platonic. When I finally mustered the gall to ask her if she kissed her last boyfriend and if she ever intended to kiss again, she gave me a tremendous relief by answering yes to both questions.

In short, Carol was asking me if I was capable of having a relationship with her without being as intimate as I would like to be with her. That concept so intrigued and challenged me that I decided I'd try. Week after week, we dated without kissing. But a day didn't go by that I didn't wake up and wonder, "Will today be the day?" I wondered what kind of reasons were holding Carol back, and what kind of relationship we'd have to have before she believed the time was right. I knew her better and better, yet I didn't know her as I longed to know her.

Jesus, it seems to me, asked Isaiah, John, and now me to have a relationship with him without the intimacy of his physical presence. At the same time, the expectancy with which I wait for that intimacy should be daily, even passionate. It will be hard to sustain that expectancy, but I want to try. At least I've had some practice. I never did kiss Carol.

What are you waiting for?

What are the events that you're eagerly anticipating in the coming days? How about in the coming year? Could the feeling you have about those things be applied to Jesus' return? Why would you want to model your expectancy after certain or promised rewards rather than long-shot dreams?

You might also take a look at . . . Isaiah 11:1-10; Revelation 1:9-18

Passing along your faith is sort of like...

Tombstone Tipping

How important a role has your family played in cultivating your faith? What role will you play for your family and generations to come?

Until my parents' generation, most of my ancestors lived and died within a hundred-mile radius. As I discovered this during conversations with my grandparents, we decided to take a couple of excursions to cemeteries near their house. Within ten miles we found the grave of my great-great-great-grandfather, who was born in 1776. Nearby was the church where his son was a founding leader. We worshiped there the next Sunday, on Father's Day.

My other grandma lived about fifty miles away. Though she was in her late eighties at the time, she too ventured out to the local country cemetery with my dad, my sister, my wife and our two children, and me. The four generations of us wandered through the graves of three generations prior to my grandma, and I thought historic thoughts about the church next to the cemetery and the faith my great-great-great-grandfather and I shared. There with our seven generations together, this place seemed to represent such permanence, such a special heritage. How many days and nights and years and decades had that tombstone stood fast? How many more decades would it bear testimony to the ancestry of a Christian family?

I turned to notice another tombstone, newer and larger than my grandfather's. It seemed to have come partially unearthed at its foundation, and was tipped slightly backwards. Curiously, I touched my foot lightly to the marble monument, sure that I'd be unable to budge anything in a place this timeless. Then the whole tombstone tipped over.

> *These commandments that I give you today are to be upon your hearts. Impress them on your children. Talk about them when you sit at home and when you walk along the road, when you lie down and when you get up. Tie them as symbols on your hands and bind them on your foreheads. Write them on the doorframes of your houses and on your gates.*
> (Deuteronomy 6:6-9)

Moses told the Israelite families that God's Word didn't dwell in a geographical place, but in the human heart. Tombstones tip over. Monuments erode. Even churches deteriorate over time.

At the same time, it's appropriate to use symbols and history as reminders and teachers. Moses not only said to impress and talk about God's commandments, he said tie them, bind them, write them. In other words, create visual object lessons that testify to God's historical faithfulness and unchanging standards.

As my dad and I tried in vain to lift the tombstone I'd tipped over, my sister and my grandma got tickled and started laughing. My dad and I, who had been grunting and barking instructions back and forth, looked at each other, considered the futility of our task, and started laughing too.

In the meantime, my wife pulled out the video camera we'd brought with us and started taping the whole thing. Many times since then, we've pulled out that videotape and recreated the afternoon when Grandma and the rest of us went tombstone tipping in Great-Great-Great-Grandpa's backyard. We created another cross-generational memory that will continue to live more in our hearts than in a country cemetery.

How steady are your tombstones?

Do the places from which you've learned about God seem rich

with heritage or hollow from empty tradition? Are you grounded as well as you'd like to be with historical roots of faith? What can you do to start making sure your heritage is coming from living hearts rather than meaningless monuments?

You might also take a look at... Psalm 90:1-12; 2 Timothy 1:5-7

God the Holy Spirit is
sort of like...

A Computer Tutor

How would you describe the Holy Spirit's role in your life? Are you letting him play the complete role that the Bible says he's willing to play?

Computers used to really intimidate me. I'd always hear people talk about how easy they were to use, and about how much I'd love using one. But usually when I asked someone to help me learn, they'd do one of two things that only made the intimidation worse.

Some people would simply point me to the computer and say "the only way you'll really learn is by doing it yourself." Then they'd hand me a computer manual as thick as the New York City phone book, and assure me that everything I needed to know was in there. I'd learn very little.

Other people would sit down at their computer, turn it on, and start typing away. They'd talk about what they were doing. They'd point to what they were doing. They'd make various noises that indicated they were puzzled, having fun, or being impressed with what they were doing. They'd ask me if I had any questions. I'd learn very little.

151

I guess I can understand why those people approached teaching that way. Maybe they were still learning themselves. Maybe they didn't have much time to spend with me. Maybe they'd forgotten what it's like to be a novice. If you're not getting paid or don't have a personal interest in the learning taking place, maybe you just look for the easiest way.

"I have much more to say to you, more than you can now bear. But when he, the Spirit of truth, comes, he will guide you into all truth. He will not speak on his own; he will speak only what he hears, and he will tell you what is yet to come. He will bring glory to me by taking from what is mine and making it known to you." (John 16:12-14)

I finally learned how to use a computer when my friend Jo Ann sat me down at one, pulled up a chair alongside me, and helped me know what to do. It was me running the computer, me making the decisions, me making an occasional mistake. It was my friend who encouraged, corrected, advised, and as a result taught me. I learned a lot that day.

One of the words the Bible uses to describe the Holy Spirit means "one called alongside." In essence, he is our personal tutor in Christlikeness. He doesn't hand us God's mysterious Word and say "good luck." He doesn't shove us aside and live our lives for us while we look over his shoulder. He comes alongside us, encourages us, advises us, in matters infinitely more important than operating a computer.

The Holy Spirit can be infinitely successful as a tutor for the same reasons my first computer teachers weren't successful. He's not still learning anything. He has all the time in the world to spend with me. He knows what it's like to be a novice—he lives in one. Also, because of his personal interest in me, he's never, ever taken the easy way out.

Are you being tutored?

Who was the best teacher or tutor you've ever had? What might be the significance of the Holy Spirit being alongside rather than in front of you or behind you? Today, how might you more effectively accept the Holy Spirit's role as a spiritual tutor?

You might also take a look at... John 14:25-26; 1 Corinthians 2:12-13

Fickle faith is sort of like...

Praying for Your Stereo

Have you ever prayed really hard for something, only to find God doesn't seem to answer? Are there times when you wonder whether your prayers should be more persistent or whether they're wrong and should stop?

During my first year of college, my stereo broke, and I had to send it off to the manufacturer for repair. It was supposed to be back in a week or so, but two weeks passed, then three, then four. Each week, I'd walk downtown to the store that had mailed it in for me and check to see if it had been returned. Each week I'd walk back to my painfully quiet dorm room, disappointed at having to do without this musical oasis amidst the desert of studying and writing papers.

This was also a time in my life when I was running from God. I wasn't sure I believed everything my parents had taught me about him, and I wasn't sure he deserved to be Lord of my life. To encourage me, my dad had mailed me a book about faith. It had amazing stories in it about people who lived daring lives of total dependence on God. They'd face impossible odds, pray to God for a specific solution, and God would respond just as they'd asked. It all seemed too easy.

So I decided to put God to the test. If he was really all my parents said he was, and if he really wanted my attention and my life, surely he could prove it to me by answering my specific prayer as he apparently had those in the faith book. I prayed for my stereo to be ready the very next Saturday, six weeks after it was supposed to have been in. After diligent, daily praying for a solid week, I went downtown believing God might show himself strong by delivering my stereo. It wasn't there.

> *Jesus answered, "I tell you the truth, you are looking for me, not because you saw miraculous signs but because you ate the loaves and had your fill. Do not work for food that spoils, but for food that endures to eternal life, which the Son of Man will give you. On him God the Father has placed his seal of approval."*
>
> *Then they asked him, "What must we do to do the works God requires?"*
>
> *Jesus answered, "The work of God is this: to believe in the one he has sent."*
>
> *So they asked him, "What miraculous sign then will you give that we may see it and believe you? What will you do?"* (John 6:26-30)

My prayer for my stereo's return wasn't a new one to God. The people that surrounded Jesus were also interested in his proving himself by granting their selfish requests. Jesus' answer then was much as it was to me while I continued to wait for my stereo. Don't seek God for what he can do for you, seek him for who he is. Don't pursue selfish goals with greater and greater diligence, pursue knowledge of God himself and understanding of what his goals are.

Faith is not merely believing with all your might that God will do something you want him to do. In the children's story *The Little Engine That Could,* the little engine gets up the side of the mountain by chugging "I think I can, I think I can" all the way. That's not faith, that's effort. The Bible even contrasts it with faith and calls it "works."

The problem with "believing with all my might" is that it's

my might I'm counting on, and my sin-tainted will that determines what I want to happen. Faith is different than that. Faith has God as its object, and knowledge of his will and purposes as its goal. When I'm "believing with all my might," I'm trying to get God to honor my plans. When I exercise true faith, I'm getting in line with his plans.

Has your stereo arrived yet?

Have you ever asked God to prove himself to you by answering a specific prayer? Do you see how he might consider that presumptuous? Could you pray today in a way that seeks God as a person?

You might also take a look at . . . Ephesians 2:8-9; Hebrews 11:1

Security is sort of like . . .

Being Safe in the Car

Do you have any doubts about the security of your relationship with God? Do you ever feel less than safe in his care?

My wife, Beth, needed to drop something off at the house of a friend who lived out in the country. She took our baby son, Caleb, with her, who was less than two years old at the time. Caleb was asleep in his car seat when they arrived, so Beth decided to leave him in the car while she ran her delivery to the door. The car doors were locked, and Caleb was sleeping, well, like a baby.

Once at the door, however, Beth found that her friend was on the phone. As her friend motioned her inside, Beth looked back at the car hesitantly. They were way out in the country, no one was around, the doors were locked, Caleb was sound asleep—it seemed fine to step inside until her friend got off the phone.

Beth was inside for only a minute or two, but when she stepped back outside she was horrified by what she saw. The family's two large dogs had emerged from the backyard, and were leaping at the car window and barking at Caleb, who by this time was no longer asleep. He was screaming and crying at the top of his lungs, looking around desperately for help, yet unable to move from the safety of his car seat.

The dogs were quickly subdued and put behind a fence. Beth pulled Caleb out of his car seat, and with tears of her own tried to explain through his terror what had happened. She talked to Caleb about how she would never leave him or endanger him. She told him the dogs couldn't possibly have entered the car. She told him they were nice dogs who wouldn't hurt him. But he still kept crying, and wouldn't let go of his mommy.

> *"I give them eternal life, and they shall never perish; no one can snatch them out of my hand. My Father, who has given them to me, is greater than all; no one can snatch them out of my Father's hand."* (John 10:28-29)

It was only natural for Caleb to be frightened. He couldn't fully understand the security that was his. He didn't really understand that the dogs couldn't get in. He didn't really understand that Mommy was close by and returning soon. His fear was as real as his safety.

It was also natural for Caleb to doubt his mommy's reassurances. He didn't have her perspective on things. He didn't have her power over the dogs. He didn't have her understanding of how long a couple of minutes is. His doubt was as real as his safety.

In other words, Caleb had fear and doubt for many of the same reasons you and I can have fear and doubt. Our circumstances can become difficult, and our perspective is limited. In the terror of the moment, we can lose track of the security we have in God's promises that nothing can separate us from his love and care.

Eventually, Caleb was comforted, calmed down, and assured. What did it take? Removing the dogs helped some. Explaining to Caleb that he was never actually in danger helped some. The real comfort came, however, in the presence of the one who loved him, even though the dogs could still be heard yapping nearby.

Are the dogs yapping at your car?

What circumstances might you face today that would lead you to fear or doubt God's promises, or even his love and protection? What has God promised you about your security, even when things get tough? How could living consistently in God's presence help you when the dogs come?

You might also take a look at... John 20:19-20; 2 Timothy 1:7-8

DAY 61

*Loving confrontation
is sort of like ...*

A Torn Paper Dress

Have you ever had to tell someone something she or he didn't like or didn't want to hear? Was it worth it?

Having raised four children and having been a junior high librarian much of her life, my mother has always made a gallant effort to be reasonably up-to-date on teenage fashion. This has occasionally led to some embarrassment on my part, but still I admire her effort to relate to her students in this way.

It's not easy for an adult to dress fashionably for junior high, especially over the course of twenty or thirty years. Mom has watched straight-legged jeans go to bell-bottom jeans and back again. She's looked over shoulders covered with long hair and over mohawk haircuts towering taller than she is. I guess I should be grateful she didn't embrace every fashion fad that came along.

In one instance, even before I was a teenager, I can remember her purchasing a "paper dress" because they were the "in thing" and she was supposed to speak to a high school group at church. For some reason I went with her and was sitting on the front row with her as she awaited her turn on the program. As she leaned forward, I noticed what I presume is one of the reasons paper dresses didn't stay in fashion for very long. It had a gaping tear straight down the back.

I considered my options. I could slip quietly to another seat and pretend I didn't know her when the snickers started; I could ask her if she had a stapler or a few paper clips; or I could tell her she was about to embarrass herself—and me, too—if she didn't do something.

> *Brothers, if someone is caught in a sin, you who are spiritual should restore him gently. But watch yourself, or you also may be tempted. Carry each other's burdens, and in this way you will fulfill the law of Christ.* (Galatians 6:1-2)

It's easy to avoid loving confrontation. We don't want to incur people's wrath, so we let them pursue a destructive behavior, hoping they'll come to their senses before the damage is too great. Surely someone will say something to them, we think. Surely they'll change direction before it gets too bad. Then they step off a cliff, and our smugness at having predicted the outcome becomes a poor substitute for knowing we were the one that perhaps could have helped them.

Paul told the Galatian Christians that loving confrontation was critical to their health. We're all imperfect travelers down a narrow road of faith, and there will always be those who wander off toward the ditch. When that happens, the solution is neither to criticize their misstep nor to pretend we haven't noticed it. We are to gently point out not just the error of their way, but the correct route back to the safe path. Carrying one another's burden means taking responsibility for one another's spiritual safety. Speaking the truth in love beats remaining silent while a fellow Christian pursues self-destruction.

When I told my mom her paper dress was risking a rip-roaring reception, she gratefully sent me to the car to retrieve a light jacket she had brought "just in case." She was able to confess to the audience that she had probably stretched her daring fashion spirit a little too far, and it had torn. The loving intervention worked. It had a happy ending. When I later kidded her about the embarrassment I had saved her and told her she owed me one, she simply told me to zip my pants up and we could call it even.

Are your friends wearing torn dresses?

Do you have any friends who are toying with dangerous habits or behaviors? What would be the risks of confronting them about those? How and when would you go about it? Is the danger they're headed toward worth risking conflict in your relationship? Is it worth risking the end of that relationship?

You might also take a look at . . . 2 Corinthians 10:8-11; 2 Thessalonians 3:11-15

A Little Brother's Apology

When is it hardest to forgive someone? Is it the offending person who makes forgiveness so difficult or something within ourselves?

Brothers, I've found, tend to pick at one another. I remember one time in particular when my younger brother Carey and I had spent most of an evening in mutual sibling provocation. Somehow it got a little out of hand, and Carey did something—I don't even remember what now—that merited parental intervention. My mother insisted that he tell me he was sorry.

Have you ever had someone make you say you're sorry when you really weren't? You'd think she had asked him to cut off his right arm. He simply refused. Never before then and never since have I seen my little brother so dug in on something. My mother insisted. She pleaded. She threatened. Eventually the entire family was drawn in to the drama, with each one trying to think of some creative incentive to coax the simple words "I'm sorry" out of this little boy.

We were missing a favorite television show. Dad got involved. An early bedtime was promised. A spanking was threatened. I was sure that withholding college tuition was next on the list, so I started pleading with him too. The spanking and bedtime came. The apology never did.

> *For if you forgive men when they sin against you, your heavenly Father will also forgive you. But if you do not forgive men their sins, your Father will not forgive your sins.*
> (Matthew 6:14-15)

Why do we choose to live in broken relationship rather than forgive one another? What's so distasteful about humbling ourselves to each other in repentance and forgiveness?

The Bible makes it clear that there are serious consequences to withholding forgiveness. The primary consequence seems to be the inability to accept forgiveness ourselves.

Because this is true, the refusal to forgive is one of the greatest dangers in the Christian's life. That refusal becomes a hindrance in our relationship with God because it creates blockage in the ongoing cycle of repentance and forgiveness that keeps clear our path to God. How far can we get in our growing relationship with him if we've no room to accept his forgiveness day by day?

I know my little brother forgave me eventually. But to this day it puzzles me that a wrong that neither of us can remember created a night of enmity that I haven't yet forgotten.

You're not holding back, are you?

Do you have any currently broken relationships? Are they broken because someone hasn't forgiven you, or because you haven't forgiven them? Could you make that right today?

You might also take a look at... Matthew 18:21-35; Mark 11:25-26

DAY 63

Rebellion is sort of like...

Hiding Under the Bed

Have you ever done something as an act of rebellion or defiance that, in retrospect, was incredibly stupid?

I had been banished to my room, and I was mad. Even though I was only eight or nine years old, I was pretty sure I had tolerated enough parental supervision in my lifetime. I felt they didn't respect me, didn't understand me, didn't give me enough freedom. It was time to show them. I'd run away from home.

As I sat in my room and plotted out the next few days and weeks of life on my own, however, I cooled down just a little and a small dose of rational thinking seeped in. I couldn't really pull off the big run-away this year, but maybe I could still teach my parents a lesson. I opened the window and screen in my room wide enough to make it look like I had crawled out. Then I wrote my parents a scathing farewell note, expressing all my frustrations and telling them they'd finally blown it by sending me to my room one time too many. I left the note by the window, then crawled under the bed.

A half hour went by, then an hour, then two. Finally I began to get cramped, claustrophobic, and tired of inhaling dust balls. I gave up on the lesson I was supposedly teaching them, crawled out, and cooled down. Soon I was released from my room and restored to a right relationship with my parents.

It was probably five years later as we were packing up our stuff to move to another town that my older brother found the note I had written, buried in the bottom of a box. Apparently it had blown there off of the windowsill that day, and I hardly remembered writing it. With great glee and marvelous dramatic expression, however, my older brother read my venomous words aloud for the whole family's amusement. Somehow those words didn't sound as noble and elegant as when I had penned them five years ago in a fit of rage and rebellion.

> *"The son said to him, 'Father, I have sinned against heaven and against you. I am no longer worthy to be called your son.'*
>
> *"But the father said to his servants, 'Quick! Bring the best robe and put it on him. Put a ring on his finger and sandals on his feet. Bring the fattened calf and kill it. Let's have a feast and celebrate. For this son of mine was dead and is alive again; he was lost and is found.' So they began to celebrate."*
> (Luke 15:21-24)

True freedom isn't merely having the independence to do

whatever you want. The son in the above story demonstrates that. True love isn't seeking to control the one you love. The father in the story demonstrates that. But when my selfishness convinces me that freedom is independence from the one who loves me, the result is usually rebellion.

Outright rebellion can create some pretty stupid actions. The prodigal son took his inheritance and blew it. I wrote a silly note and hid under my bed for two hours. He cooled down in a pigpen. I cooled down under a bed. His father welcomed him home lovingly. My parents showed the same love in releasing me from my room as they had in sending me there.

How's life under the bed?

What freedoms do you really want that might be wrong or at least premature? Can you see down the road how the desire for those freedoms might lead to rebellion? What advance steps might you take that could help you avoid the explosion into rebellion?

You might also take a look at... Daniel 9:4-9; Romans 6:15-18

Caring for people is sort of like ...

Getting to Know the "Unknown"

Are there people around you who are "anonymous," who you see all the time but don't really know? How much do you have to know about someone to share the love of God with him or her?

At the school where my wife and I met, I was a little more of a public figure than she was. More people knew me than knew her because she was reserved and quiet and, well, I wasn't. She still jokes that she's known by more people as my wife than as Beth.

Actually, Beth's never tried very hard to shed her anonymity. There's something secure and nice about not being singled out, especially if you're basically shy. She's taught me something about the comfort of staying in the shadows, and I've taught her a little about handling the spotlight where I sometimes drag her.

When a choir from the school came to sing at our church, however, I was sure that they would know Beth and Beth would know them better than I would. I had never had a class with the choir director, but Beth had. As the director came up the aisle to greet us, you could tell she remembered us.

"Why hello, Nate, it's so good to see you!" she beamed. She went on to ask a couple of polite questions about what I was doing now and where we lived, etc. Then she turned to Beth, knew we went together, but obviously drew a blank on her name.

"Why, hello ... there, it's good to see you too!" was her gracious response to the awkward moment. She then relieved us all by moving on quickly to another conversation. Ever since then, Beth has kidded that I should just introduce her that way: "Hello, my name is Nate, and this is my wife, There."

> Then, leaving her water jar, the woman went back to the town and said to the people, "Come, see a man who told me everything I ever did. Could this be the Christ?" They came out of the town and made their way toward him.
> (John 4:28-30)

The awkward encounter between my wife and the choir director wasn't that unusual. There are lots of people in our lives who we barely know, and lots of people who barely know us. Usually, we're content to leave it that way, to rub past each other with an impersonal "Hi there." It gets us past the awkward encounter, and we never have to go any deeper into their lives, or let them any deeper into ours.

The "woman at the well" could be pretty sure she didn't know Jesus. Left to her own initiative, she never would have. He was a Jew and she was a Samaritan, and the two never associated if they could help it. However, what should have passed quickly as an awkward "Hi ... there" moment was turned by Jesus into a deep conversation.

Imagine meeting someone for the first time and having him tell you things you felt he had no way of knowing. The woman who met Jesus at the well was defensive and evasive until Jesus showed that he knew and cared about her personally. Before then, their conversation was about water, about the day's work, about religion. But by the time she went to tell others about Jesus, she described him as someone who knew her intimately.

I have lots of "Hi there" people in my life. I doubt I'll ever get past superficial talk about the weather with them until I take the time to know them personally. I wonder if getting to know them personally will give me a chance to bring them to the well?

It's there they can meet my friend Jesus, who knows them intimately already.

Ready to meet a few "theres"?

How many acquaintances can you think of whose full names you do not know? Are there people who know your name and look up to you, yet you haven't given them much thought? How could you channel their respect for you into an introduction to God? Will you have an opportunity today?

You might also take a look at . . . Jeremiah 1:4-5; Psalm 139

*Sharing your faith is
sort of like . . .*

Wanting to Have "Friends Forever"

How many of your best friends aren't Christians? Would talking candidly with them about your relationship with God jeopardize any of those friendships?

I attended two colleges and had a best friend in each one. At the first college there weren't many Christians, and my best friend didn't know God personally. I attended that college during a time when I had distanced myself from God, too. I had been a Christian since I was a young boy, but was not letting God be boss of my life.

It was during my freshman year at that first college that God's stubborn love reached out to me and showed me he deserved to be Lord of my life. I then transferred to another college the next year to help rebuild my shaky spiritual foundation. There I found a new best friend who was a Christian.

I couldn't forget my friend from the first college, however. As I made more and more friends with whom I knew I'd spend eternity, I frequently thought of my friend who didn't know God personally. I couldn't get away from the thought that, unless something changed, this good friend would be eternally separated from God. Perhaps my motive was selfish, but I wanted him to share heaven with me.

After we graduated, my friend and I continued to live several hundred miles apart, but a business trip my first year out of school gave me the opportunity to spend a weekend with him again. Throughout the weekend, I shared my faith in the most passionate, intense way I ever have. He needed to know the Lord. I needed him to know the Lord. I needed to know our friendship wouldn't end at death.

Just before he drove me to the airport, we spent three hours in a pizza place. In the most direct, heartfelt way I could, I explained one more time what Christ had done in my life and how he could do it for my friend as well. He listened carefully and said that I was the only genuine Christian he had personally known. That humbled and hurt me when I realized how weak my example had been during the year we had spent together. Still, he said he didn't sense God was real for him. As he dropped me off at the airport, asking him to accept Christ was my parting plea. He said no.

> *Then Agrippa said to Paul, "Do you think that in such a short time you can persuade me to be a Christian?"*
>
> *Paul replied, "Short time or long—I pray God that not only you but all who are listening to me today may become what I am, except for these chains."* (Acts 26:28-29)

It continues to break my heart when I think about my friend not knowing Christ, but I've had a peace since that pizza dinner that I didn't have before it. Up until that time, I had the haunting knowedge that I had never told my good friend the truth about God.

I suppose that back when my friend and I were in college, I could have argued that he could see God in my life, regardless of whether I spoke about him. In fact, he confirmed that truth during our last conversation. But if we hadn't had that talk, I would never have known for sure whether I had been clear in my testimony to him. Now, even though my heart aches for my friend to know Christ, I know he's heard the truth. I know that he'll never have to wonder why his best friend didn't tell him.

Are your friends "friends forever"?

Which of your close friends have never heard the message of salvation? Are you counting on them to notice the testimony of your life without having to hear the testimony of your lips? Is there one of them you can start praying for today? Are you willing for that prayer to lead to action?

You might also take a look at . . . 1 Corinthians 7:29-31; 2 Timothy 4:1-5

DAY 66

God the Son is sort of like . . .

Butch Cassidy and the Sundance Kid

Have you thought much about the mystery of eternal God becoming mortal man? How important is it that Jesus is fully God and fully man?

As a young boy, I loved westerns. One of my earliest memories is of strapping on my holster and toy gun, putting on my badge and cowboy hat, and watching Roy Rogers

while astride the big armchair that was my trusty steed. As Roy chased bad guys at full gallop, I would bounce up and down on that arm chair, shooting at the television screen and trying not to wing Roy in the process.

As I grew older, Roy was replaced as my western hero by the Lone Ranger. I felt sort of bad abandoning Roy, but the Ranger had a better horse and a real Indian sidekick instead of a girl. Plus, the Lone Ranger had that cool mask. I still remember the time my dad bought me one like it at the local dime store. When I wore it in the school yard the next morning it incited a riot of forty or fifty kids, who chased me all over the playground just to find out, "Who is that masked man?"

On from the Lone Ranger to Clint Eastwood and others, the image of the mysterious western hero continued to fascinate me. One of my favorite movie scenes is in Butch Cassidy and the Sundance Kid where Robert Redford and Paul Newman are being chased on horseback after robbing a train. No matter how hard they ride or what evasive maneuver they pull, their pursuers keep coming.

Butch and The Kid aren't used to this kind of pursuit. They've always been skilled and clever enough to escape capture for their previous crimes, and never had to work very hard at it. Now their best efforts aren't shaking loose the tenacious, seemingly supernatural group that's following them. Each time they cover their trail, ride through a stream, jump on the same horse, or ride up a mountain, they look back, see their pursuers gaining on them, and ask, "Who are those guys?"

> *"I told you that you would die in your sins; if you do not believe that I am the one I claim to be, you will indeed die in your sins."*
>
> *"Who are you?" they asked.*
>
> *"Just what I have been claiming all along," Jesus replied.*
> (John 8:24-25)

The skeptics hanging around Jesus were having the same trouble Butch Cassidy and the Sundance Kid were having, and the same trouble the Lone Ranger's adversaries had. They were seeing something they had never seen before, something that seemed supernatural, and it puzzled them. Their question was the same as Butch's and The Kid's: "Who is this guy?"

Both Jesus' skeptics and our western movie villains suffered from an inflated view of themselves and an underestimation of whom they were dealing with. Butch and The Kid presumed they were dealing with a mere posse. Jesus' skeptics presumed they were dealing with a mere man.

There's nothing more critical to understand about Jesus than the fact that he is who he said he is. He is fully God and fully man. Jesus' skeptics said they believed in God, but they were unwilling to believe he would take on human form. They undoubtedly believed Jesus was a man, but they couldn't accept his claim to be supernatural, even though everything he did pointed to that truth.

If Jesus isn't God, he doesn't have the authority to deal with our sin. If he isn't human—not just back then, but now—he hasn't lived a perfect life and conquered death and the grave to satisfy God's holy demands.

Who is this guy? Just who he's been claiming to be all along.

Who is this guy?

Do you think of Jesus as being fully God, or does he seem like a great hero that lived a long time ago? Do you think of Jesus as fully man, or does he seem like a supernatural ghost that can walk through walls but isn't like you and me? How might it change your relationship with him today to concentrate on who he said he is?

You might also take a look at... John 1:14-18; Hebrews 2:9-18

Devotion to God is sort of like . . .

A Family Resemblance

Which member of your family do you physically look the most like? Which member of your family do you act the most like?

Some of my earliest memories are as a preschool child, going on errands with my father. We'd go to the post office, the dry cleaner's, or the bank, and I'd parade in at his side—actually at the side of his kneecap. The very large people behind each one of those counters would inevitably pinch my cheek or rub my head and say basically the same thing: "My, my, my, you look just like your dad!"

These experiences gave me the early delusion that large people who work behind counters are stupid because I knew I didn't look anything like my dad! He was six feet six inches tall, well over 220 pounds, and had a receding hairline. I was probably three feet tall, fifty pounds, and had hair. How could they say we looked alike?

Although I was convinced of their stupidity or nearsightedness, I was at the same time very, very proud of the comparison. My dad was the largest living human I had ever seen, the apple of my eye, and capable of anything my preschool mind could think of. Best of all, he actually seemed to like me! I occasionally got the notion that I was the apple of his eye as well! So even if those people were loony, the idea that I was even faintly like him made me beam.

As I grew older, I have to admit there were years when the comparison didn't mean as much to me. The bigger my little boy world got, the more heroes and models I found. Dad began losing ground to sports heroes, rock stars, and eventually to millionaire businessmen and powerful leaders.

But Dad stayed pretty consistent while my heroes paraded by and gradually earned my disenchantment. Now here I am again, treasuring the comparison, and wondering if it can ever be true.

> *How great is the love the Father has lavished on us, that we should be called children of God! And that is what we are! The reason the world does not know us is that it did not know him. Dear friends, now we are children of God, and what we will be has not yet been made known. But we know that when he appears, we shall be like him, for we shall see him as he is. Everyone who has this hope in him purifies himself, just as he is pure.* (1 John 3:1-3)

The idea that we have been made God's own children, his own dear kids, is enough to overwhelm you if you think about it. What lavish love that would make the creator of the universe adopt vagabonds like us! And part of what goes with the father-child deal is an ever-increasing family resemblance. In the same way our human genetics help us look like our parents, our new spiritual genetics help us to look more and more like our heavenly Father.

But you know, I didn't stop with just the genetics in trying to look like my father. That little preschool boy would put on Daddy's shoes, wrap himself in Daddy's belt (several times), and comb his hair with Daddy's comb. I was overjoyed to naturally look like him, but I also wanted to "put on" his look externally.

That must be what John means when he says that we Christians who have hope of being like God one day are also busy now, "purifying ourselves, just as he is pure." After all, we want all the people behind the counters in our lives to notice the resemblance.

Some of my favorite song lyrics, written by Wayne Watson, express this sentiment:

One day Jesus will call my name.
As days go by, I hope I don't stay the same.
I want to get so close to him, that it's no big change,
On that day that Jesus calls my name.

Do you look like your father?

Who are the people you know who, spiritually, look most like God? Why did you think of them? In what ways is the resemblance clear? If you wanted to look more like God today than you did yesterday, how would you begin? Will you begin?

You might also take a look at... 2 Corinthians 3:18; Ephesians 5:1-2

DAY 68

God's grace is sort of like . . .

Eggplant Casserole

Have you ever tasted something you thought you hated and discovered you liked it? Has your spiritual life ever worked that same way?

There are many foods I don't care for much, but there are a couple that I really detest. I'm not talking about foods that are a little tough to chew or not quite done. I'm talking about foods whose very aroma makes me want to ... well, you get the idea.

One day when my grandmother brought out a mushy looking dish and called it eggplant casserole, I decided to

173

politely decline. I knew I was prejudging this bowl-o-mush, because I didn't even know what an eggplant looked like, or what other plant might have laid it. But it sounded like something that could be in that nauseating category if you thought too much about it, and looked like something that had already been eaten once.

I don't know if your grandmother is like my grandmother, but mine isn't the type of person you say no to very easily. She's a gentle, southern lady from western Kentucky whose soft drawl could melt butter. But don't tell her you don't want to eat her eggplant casserole.

Reluctantly, almost gagging, I spooned in a microscopic bite. You guessed it, I vomited in my plate. No, no, I'm kidding. I liked it—a lot! It's now become one of the "favorite foods" that's often brought to holiday meals in our family. And of course, it can't be served without the ceremonial reminder that I once refused to eat a bite of it.

Taste and see that the Lord is good; blessed is the man who takes refuge in him. (Psalm 34:8)

What is it in our nature that gives us a predisposition to hate something before we've tried it? In the case of eggplant casserole, I think the reason was twofold. First, I presumed to have knowledge of something about which I was ignorant. Second, I didn't want to be told what to do. More than I didn't want to taste eggplant, I wanted to exercise my will to choose what would or wouldn't get past my lips.

Many people assume they know what God is like. They assume they know the demands of the Christian faith, and they characterize it as unpleasant, restrictive, or nonsensical. Most of all, they want to control what goes past the lips of their life. They want to retain their self-will at all costs.

Such stubbornness isn't reserved for nonbelievers, either. How many times has God revealed something new to me or shown me some area of obedience or disobedience with which I need to deal? And how many times have I dismissed it as too hard or too distasteful, when in reality I'm simply saying I don't want to try it.

My grandmother's persistence is nothing compared to God's. He keeps serving up the same dish of grace over and over and over again until I've agreed to taste and see that he is good and that he knows what's best for me. In the end, the eggplant casserole principle holds true. The very thing that seemed so distasteful at first becomes one of my spirit's most tasteful blessings.

Eating your vegetables?

What are the areas of spiritual obedience or disobedience that seem most distasteful to you these days? In your situation, what would a "taste" of God's way mean? Will you try some today?

You might also take a look at... Psalm 119:103; Hebrews 6:4-6

Coveting is sort of like...

Winning Snakes at the Carnival

Do you ever struggle with wanting what other people have? Is coveting usually an intentional decision, or does it just sort of happen to you?

The carnival that was set up in a park near our house each spring always brought a unique combination of excitement and shadiness to our neighborhood. It was full of lights and smells and games and rides, but its workers were strangers to us, who seemed crafty, almost sinister. They arrived out of nowhere, and you never really saw them leave. This may have added to my suspicion of the carnival, but rarely kept me away from it.

When I was young I'd go to the carnival mainly for the rides, but in high school I was more interested in the carnival as a place to go on a date. You could still enjoy the rides, but now the terror of their centrifugal motion could be used for the additional benefit of having your date slide into your side and hold on tight in either real or pretended fear.

Then there was the whole trap of winning stuffed animals. It seemed every other couple walking around at the carnival consisted of a girl holding one or more huge stuffed animals and a guy strutting at her side as if he had just medaled in an Olympic event. This of course sent the girls who weren't holding such trophies into ooohs of envy that obliged their accompanying males and their egos to go win some for their dates.

The year after I first noticed and cared about this phenomenon, I was planning to take a very special date to the carnival. I decided to go over there a night early to scout out the rides and find the game where my odds were greatest at winning things. That year, the popular trophies were long stuffed snakes. The girls were wearing them around their necks, over their arms, and around their waists. The tragic thing about this new fad was that one snake wasn't enough! The ooohs I heard weren't just over having a snake, they were over how many snakes other girls were wearing or carrying.

I decided I needed to practice. At an undersized basketball hoop with an oversized basketball, I spent ten dollars and won one snake. I was in trouble. Most everyone who knew me knew I played on the basketball team, and I hardly went to a carnival any more where some of my acquaintances didn't goad me into proving I could shoot as well at the carnival as on the court. I spent another five dollars and won one more snake.

The next night, with the added pressure and incentive of my date at my side, I was able to spend fifteen dollars and win three snakes—enough to walk around the carnival with the minimum daily requirement of respect. When I got home, however, I couldn't escape the thought that I had spent thirty dollars to be able to carry three snakes for three hours. Later I would see my snake friends glaring at me from a toy store shelf, a one-dollar sale tag hanging from their sinister smiles.

> *But godliness with contentment is great gain. For we brought nothing into the world, and we can take nothing out of it. But if we have food and clothing, we will be content with that. People who want to get rich fall into temptation and a trap and into many foolish and harmful desires that plunge men into ruin and destruction.* (1 Timothy 6:6-9)

Coveting, like so many vices, begins when we compare ourselves to others. We then complicate our envy with an inaccurate assessment of what's really valuable. We think it's whatever they have and we don't. Then, as we desire those things, we're lured into methods for fulfilling those desires that are destructive.

It wouldn't have been easy to walk around the carnival and not want the snakes of status others had. It would have been even harder to want them and not go try to win one, even in a jaded game of small rims and large basketballs.

What should I have done? I guess I should have focused on being grateful for what I had rather than worrying about what others had. Because now that I think back on the experience, one thing I did have to be grateful for was a date who never even asked me to win her a snake.

How much are your snakes costing?

What are the symbols of status your friends have that allure you the most? Have you ever thought of that as what the Bible calls coveting? What might be the inflated costs of the things you find yourself wanting today? What do you think the Bible means by "godliness with contentment"? Is it worth a try?

You might also take a look at . . . Psalm 39:4-7; Luke 12:15-21

Growing faith is sort of like...

Losing Your Luggage and Learning to Love It

How much of your spiritual life is routine? Do you ever feel like you're doing religious things, yet not growing spiritually?

The one ocean cruise I've been on was a fun but rather threatening experience. It was like any trip where you have to pack up a limited amount of your life to survive on until you get home, yet the feeling of isolation was far greater. We were embarking on our own floating island, cut off from the rest of the world by miles and miles of distance and mega-gallons of ocean too infinite to count.

But my feelings of being cut off from my life were nothing compared to another guy I met on the ship. The airline had lost his luggage before he boarded. He decided to go ahead on the cruise, with the airline's promise that they would fly it to our first port for him to pick up. It didn't arrive at our first port, or our second, or our third.

During those few days when we cruised from port to port, I watched a funny transformation take place in this man. During the first couple of days I saw his rage mellow into a calmer, more rational anger. Then he seemed to settle into frustration and resignation.

And why not? Every day he was wearing the same clothes. Every day he did without the personal comforts he had carefully packed to make his cruise vacation more enjoyable. Every day he had to answer the same inane questions about whether his luggage had arrived yet, when his unchanging wardrobe made it obvious it hadn't.

After those first couple of days, though, something interesting began to happen. It was as if the adventure this man was being forced through was giving him a new, unencumbered freedom to enjoy life. Everyone else had to dress up for dinner. He wore the same flowered shirt and shorts. Everyone else knew only the few people they came with. Everyone knew and sympathized with "the guy who lost his luggage." He was the most popular guy on board.

I began to admire and even envy the way this man spent his days. He was no longer entrenched in the routines or even the comforts of the life he "packed" to bring with him. Instead, he was forced to live each new day for whatever it offered, depending on the grace and good will of others. When his luggage finally arrived, I lost track of him. He drifted back into the mass of us that lived a predictable, routine life, which we pack for security and take with us wherever we go.

> *The Lord had said to Abram, "Leave your country, your people and your father's household and go to the land I will show you. I will make you into a great nation and I will bless you; I will make your name great, and you will be a blessing. I will bless those who bless you, and whoever curses you I will curse; and all peoples on earth will be blessed through you."*
>
> *So Abram left, as the Lord had told him; and Lot went with him. Abram was seventy-five years old when he set out from Haran.* (Genesis 12:1-4)

There's something about moving out of our rituals and routines that is both refreshing and liberating. Imagine seventy-five-year-old Abram picking up and leaving his family and country to go somewhere he'd never been. For hundreds of years his family would be wandering nomads without a place to call home or a cultural routine in which to settle. But what a life of faith they lived, and what great things God did through them when they moved under his leadership rather than stagnating in the same place.

In the years that followed, Abram's descendants would occupy a land, build cities, and place the once mobile Ark of the

Covenant in a "permanent" temple. Yet as we read the Old Testament we almost get the idea that the less they moved, the less they depended on God. The more they remained in one place, the more they became settled in ritual and religion rather than relationship.

Maybe someday I'll take another cruise. If I do, I'm seriously considering taking only one outfit and no luggage.

How light are you traveling?

Do you ever let religious activity replace daily faith? Is it possible to get so caught up in routines that you lose track of what it's like to live a daring, moving life of faith? Which of your religious routines might be limiting you more than helping you grow? How could you go about abandoning yourself more to a life of dependent faith today?

You might also take a look at . . . Numbers 13:30-14:11; Psalm 55:19; John 15:1-5

180

God the Holy Spirit is sort of like . . .

Help out of the Quicksand

Have you ever been in a truly desperate situation where you really needed help? Did someone help you?

One of my earliest memories is of being on a swing set far away from the house, in someone's country backyard where my parents were visiting. My older brother and I, probably about ages five and three at the time, were playing on this old swing set at the edge of the yard near the woods.

My brother had offered to push me—in the swing that is—and I was soaring high. When he suddenly decided to go back to the house, I didn't wait for the swing to stop to go with him. I jumped out of the swing and landed, ankle-deep, in a huge mud puddle.

Fortunately, my brother saw it happen. Unfortunately, he had been watching a few too many cartoons.

"Don't move, it's quicksand!" he screamed.

Now I had watched enough cartoons to know what landing in quicksand meant—though apparently not enough to know the difference between quicksand and mud—and I knew that moving or struggling when you were in quicksand only hastened your departure into the netherworld. So I dutifully froze.

My gallant, five-year-old brother said he'd go to get help, but that if I moved he'd know it because I wouldn't be there when he got back. He left, and for what seemed like about a half hour, no one came to help me.

> *And I will ask the Father, and he will give you another Counselor to be with you forever—the Spirit of truth. The world cannot accept him, because it neither sees him nor knows him. But you know him, for he lives with you and will be in you. I will not leave you as orphans; I will come to you.* (John 14:16-18)

The Holy Spirit is God. He is God coming alongside you and me in our time of need to pull us out of quicksand, and often to pull us out of mud we only think is quicksand. We started our relationship to God through Jesus, but Jesus—God incarnate, or God in human form—has gone away for what seems like a very long time, especially when you're in the quicksand.

Jesus said he wouldn't leave us without a Counselor, a Comforter, a Helper. It's his own Spirit, God in a form so mysterious that he both lives with us and is in us, an "ever-present help in trouble," the psalmist says. The Holy Spirit helps us not just in the sense of rescue. He also helps us day by day to live obediently and become more and more like Jesus.

When my father arrived to pull me out of the quicksand, he had some words of instruction for my brother and some words of clarification for me on the difference between mud and quicksand. His role was not just to rescue me, but to instruct me and equip me in a way that helped me grow up.

Stuck in the mud?

In what ways could you use the Holy Spirit's "rescue" this week? In what ways could you use his daily help in growing spiritually? Might you be resisting his help in any way? Why?

You might also take a look at . . . Psalm 30:8-12; Hebrews 13:5-6

Watering Down the Apple Juice

Does compromise seem to burst into your life or creep in through a side entrance? Are there ever any warning signs that you're about to slip into doing something wrong?

Sometimes it's hard to believe that my two sons come from the same set of parents. Caleb has blond hair, Noah brown hair. One looks more like his mother, the other looks more like me. One started talking at a very early age, the other only grunted until he was nineteen months. While both boys are basically sweet-spirited, one is much more passive and submissive. The other has been described positively as "having personality," and not so positively as being demon-possessed. They were kidding, of course.

One thing is certain, their gastrointestinal make-up is entirely different. When they were both in diapers, Noah would often, well, create a stinky diaper three, four, sometimes five times a day. Caleb, on the other hand, could go over a week without one, but then, look out!

We discussed this inconsistency with their doctor, but his learned opinion was simply that, "every child is different." He was, however, more concerned about Caleb's, uh, "frequency" of only once every several days. Since both of the boys were drinking apple juice as their main beverage, the doctor suggested that we start diluting our "frequent" son's apple juice, and move our "less frequent" son to prune juice.

I'll spare you the specific results. Suffice it to say that potency as well as frequency was affected. For the next several days, we fine-tuned their "output" by carefully monitoring their "input." They were still very different in this and many other ways, but we were able to influence their consistency in this area by acknowledging the differences in their physical make-up.

> *I know where you live—where Satan has his throne. Yet you remain true to my name. You did not renounce your faith in me, even in the days of Antipas, my faithful witness, who was put to death in your city—where Satan lives.*
>
> *Nevertheless, I have a few things against you: You have people there who hold to the teaching of Balaam, who taught Balak to entice the Israelites to sin by eating food sacrificed to idols and by committing sexual immorality. Likewise you also have those who hold to the teaching of the Nicolaitans. Repent therefore! Otherwise, I will soon come to you and will fight against them with the sword of my mouth.* (Revelation 2:13-16)

Every child is different, and so is every Christian and every church. In the second and third chapters of Revelation, Jesus has written seven letters to seven different churches. Each church has its own unique make-up, its own set of strengths and sometimes weaknesses. Therefore Jesus has individual, tailored advice for each one.

This group of Christians, the church at Pergamum, had been watering down the truth, and the results stunk. They had remained consistent and faithful in many ways, but had allowed dangerous false teaching to take place in their midst. They had been loyal so far, but didn't recognize how their loyalty was being undermined by people who claimed to have a word from God, but didn't even know him.

For their own spiritual health, Jesus needed to change the consistency of their spiritual input. That which they had allowed to become diluted and weakened they now needed purified and made more potent. If they wouldn't do it, Jesus promised to come and do it himself.

How strong is your juice?

How would you describe the visible fruits or output of your spiritual life? How does the quality of what you feed on spiritually affect the nature of what your life produces outwardly? What could you feed your spirit that would help you please God with your life today?

You might also take a look at... Philippians 1:27; 1 Timothy 4:1-2

Pride is sort of like...

A Bad Answer on a Pop Quiz

Have you ever been tested on something and found yourself unprepared? What did you do?

My freshman history teacher had a terribly effective way of making sure we kept up with our daily reading assignments: pop quizzes. He made it clear from the beginning that on any given day of class we might have a quiz on the previous day's reading. Eventually, half of our grade was based on those quiz scores.

In reality, the quizzes came only every five to ten days. As the semester went on, most of us came up with some sort of system for gambling with our reading assignments. Once a quiz had struck, for example, we'd reason that the odds were greatly against having another one soon, so we'd be less likely to stay caught up on the reading. Every day you could "get by" without a quiz amounted to reading you didn't have to do until exam time, since the quizzes were only on the previous day's reading. Whatever we learned or didn't learn about history, we certainly made up for in mathematical probability skills.

Of course, the day came when that crafty historian did the statistically unthinkable. He gave quizzes on not two, but three days in a row. The second day hadn't caught me off guard. I had seen something deviously suspicious in his eyes, and prepared for the worst. But what kind of subhuman would give pop quizzes on three consecutive days? As I took out my sheet of paper, I had that terrible sinking feeling in my stomach. I had skimmed, but not read, the assignment. Bluffing, I decided, was my only hope.

Allow me to make the rest of a humiliating story as brief as possible. The answer to one of the questions was "The Punic Wars." As a fairly naive high school freshman, I had a lot of subjects sort of confused in my head. In the panic of the moment, the bluffed answer I wrote was, "The Pubic Wars."

I thought the feeling I had in the pit of my stomach when that quiz was announced was the worst one in the world. It was nothing, however, compared to the pain I felt as my answer was read aloud to the class by the person behind me who was grading it. He was a snickering sophomore who was supposedly asking if my "very close" answer was acceptable. But as soon as he read it,

I knew I had mixed up my history and health readings, and that my "near miss" bluff was much farther away from the truth than the one letter difference in the words.

The Lord abhors dishonest scales, but accurate weights are his delight. When pride comes, then comes disgrace, but with humility comes wisdom. (Proverbs 11:1-2)

After my embarrassing history quiz, I stopped gambling and read every assignment for the rest of the semester. That doesn't mean I've completely learned to stop bluffing, though. The same cockiness that convinced me I didn't have to read my history assignment still tells me I can get by with less than what's demanded of me, both by others and by God. That pride, as Proverbs calls it, welcomes shortcuts, deception, and bluffing as twisted alternatives to simply doing what I'm supposed to do as defined by those who have authority in my life. It affects and infects not just the history quizzes of my life, but the other more important tests where I decide I can bluff others into believing I'm something I'm not. Sometimes I'm even foolish enough to try bluffing God.

Just as Proverbs predicts, pride leads to disgrace. Fortunately for my history grade, that disgrace did not turn me sour and defiant. Instead, my disgrace brought me great humility. And that humility eventually led to wisdom—not just wisdom to improve a history grade, but wisdom to use the "accurate weights" of preparation and disciplined study instead of the "dishonest scales" of gambling and bluffing. It was a rough path to wisdom, and still is.

Finding it tough to bluff?

Do you ever find yourself leading others to believe something that's not true about you? How easy is it to perpetuate that deceit, either by things you say or things you don't say? What would be a more humble approach?

You might also take a look at . . . Genesis 12:11-20; Proverbs 20:17

*Helping others grow
spiritually is sort of like...*

Baby-sitting

*Do you ever get impatient with other Christians who
seem to be acting immaturely? How do you handle your
impatience?*

B abies, almost everyone admits, are cute. But let's be honest.
Babies for the most part are also incredibly annoying.
They're always crying or whining, usually because they
want something stuck in their front end or emptied out of their
back end. They can't walk. They can't talk. They can't do anything for themselves. Worst of all, there's painfully little you can
teach them. While babies are babies, all you can do is feed them,
change them, clean them up, and hold them.

Even once they start walking you can have all kinds of problems. When my little sister Alita was learning to walk (I was eight
or nine at the time), her favorite prancing ground was in front of
the television. Like a little wind-up doll, she'd parade back and
forth in front of some very important program, oblivious to the
frustration she was causing me. When I would kindly call this to
her attention, she'd inevitably just freeze in front of the screen
and grin at me with that "you-can't-hit-me-I'm-still-a-baby" look
that just drove me crazy. All I could do was trip her and pretend I
didn't know what happened when she cried. Even that tactic was
useless after she learned to talk a little.

Older children are much more gratifying. When I got old
enough to baby-sit my little brother and sister, I found that discipline was the key to molding them into productive members of
society. Whenever they would misbehave, I made their punish-
ment cleaning the bathrooms top to bottom. I remember with
pride the time my parents returned home to two exhausted but

obedient children and their proud big brother baby-sitter. When asked how things went, my little brother Carey simply replied, "Mom and Dad, if anything ever happened to you two, I want you to be comforted that the house would soon be spotless, and we'd soon be dead too."

> *Brothers, I could not address you as spiritual but as worldly—mere infants in Christ. I gave you milk, not solid food, for you were not yet ready for it. Indeed, you are still not ready.* (1 Corinthians 3:1-2)

Immature Christians can be a lot like babies. They may have difficulty feeding themselves on God's Word, or even acting like a Christian in the most basic ways. Sometimes their priority seems to be what feels or tastes good rather than solid nourishment. They seem to fall easily, and sometimes don't have spiritual discipline that would compare to potty training for a baby. All this comes from a lingering attachment to an environment like the mother's womb, rather than the new life that comes after a new birth.

Babies, however, need to be babies at least for a while. They need the basics, sometimes over and over. For their distasteful habits they need patient tolerance combined with encouragement to greater and greater discipline. They don't need their noses rubbed in their mistakes. The attachment to their old environment is being outgrown, and expecting new believers to be spiritual giants is as absurd as expecting a baby to drive a car.

Babies become toddlers, toddlers become children, children become teenagers, and teenagers become adults. It's only when babies stay babies for year after year that our concern for their spiritual growth should be heightened. Even then, it's God who handles the bathroom-cleanings of discipline in his house.

Growing tired of baby-sitting?

Are there Christians around you whose immaturity concerns you? Have they had enough time to be spiritual babies? Do they need more nurturing or more challenging? Do you need to be more patient and tolerant of their growth pace, or more helpful in encouraging them along? Can you remember Christians who have patiently helped you to grow?

You might also take a look at... Hebrews 5:13-14; 1 Peter 2:1-3

Being teachable is sort of like ...

Ear Day

Do you know many good listeners? Are you one of them?

My high school student council was a pretty sharp, active group, but I often wondered if the fifty of us really represented the school's three thousand students very well. The rest of the students didn't seem to care that much about the activities we were sponsoring or the causes we were supporting. So I decided to suggest an "Ear Day."

On Ear Day, everyone in the student council would wear a cardboard ear pinned or hung somewhere on his or her body. When other students would ask us why we were wearing the silly things, it gave us the opportunity to tell them we were on the student council and were interested in their opinion. We wanted to hear their concerns, their suggestions, and anything that could help us represent them better.

When I suggested the idea to the rest of the group, the response was lukewarm at best. A majority voted to do it, however, and the date was set to give Ear Day our best shot. The morning we headed out into the student body with our ears pinned on, I was proud. I was sure these fifty ears would permeate the campus, and we'd get the kind of feedback we needed to be more effective representatives.

As Ear Day wore on, I noticed the cardboard ears were being worn with some degree of cynicism and sarcasm. Some had hung earrings in them. Others had painted ear wax dripping from them. Several people were wearing them in places very difficult to notice. But what distressed me the most were the student council members who buried their ears in a notebook as soon as they walked out of the council room and didn't wear them at all.

> *"This is why I speak to them in parables: 'Though seeing, they do not see; though hearing, they do not hear or understand.' In them is fulfilled the prophecy of Isaiah: 'You will be ever hearing but never understanding; you will be ever seeing but never perceiving. For this people's heart has become calloused; they hardly hear with their ears, and they have closed their eyes. Otherwise they might see with their eyes, hear with their ears, understand with their hearts and turn, and I would heal them.' But blessed are your eyes because they see, and your ears because they hear."* (Matthew 13:13-16)

Why do some people choose not to listen when they have the opportunity? What could make listening and being teachable so unattractive? Jesus, quoting Isaiah, said that a calloused heart is the culprit. Having heard God's demands on my life, I either hear and obey or I refuse to change. Each time I refuse to change, my heart hardens. Eventually my heart can get so hard that I can't hear God's voice at all.

Some of my student council members, I know, were embarrassed to wear the cardboard ear. Others were too afraid of mockery or too shy of conversation with those they didn't know well. Later, when I asked them why they had bailed out, many council members used those excuses. But as I pressed them further, it became clear to me they all shared the same underlying motive—they didn't want to face the changes that might be required of them if they did listen.

Are you wearing your ear?

On a scale of one to ten, how teachable are you? Are you more teachable with your parents, your friends, your teachers, or God? What makes the differences between them? What role could more effective listening play today that would increase your teachability?

You might also take a look at... Ezekiel 33:30-32; Isaiah 6:9-10

DAY 76

Self-righteousness is sort of like ...

Throwing an Eraser in Typing Class

Have you ever known people who were completely wrong, but had convinced themselves that they were right? Have you ever experienced that sort of delusion yourself?

Joe sat next to me in typing class for a full semester. Joe didn't like typing class. He didn't like our typing teacher. He didn't even like typewriters. Joe is the one who would sit down to his machine before the teacher arrived and pound his large fist into the keyboard to see how many keys he could get to jam together.

Joe rarely brought his own typing paper to class, or his own typing eraser. On one particular day when the teacher had stepped out, Joe borrowed an eraser from someone across the room. This was a definite no-no, since not bringing your own typing supplies subtracted from your daily grade. When he had finished using it, he whistled to his buddy and sent the eraser flying across the room full of desks.

Just as the eraser left his hand, our teacher walked back into the room. All Joe's poor accomplice could do was catch it and smile sheepishly. The teacher wasn't after the other guy, however. She had spent the entire semester just a hair short of catching Joe in the act, and now she had him. With a smug, almost sinister smile on her face, she very deliberately and knowingly asked, "Joe, did you just throw that eraser?"

The answer was painfully obvious to everyone in the room, but you could tell she wanted to draw this moment of guilt out for her own maximum enjoyment. That's why Joe's calm answer was so shocking.

"No," was his simple reply.

All eyes turned back to Joe's accuser, who was noticeably shaken. All she could think to do was repeat the question, hoping she had somehow misphrased it or that he had misunderstood.

"Joe ..." She was quite serious now, realizing that she was on the spot. We all wanted to see how she'd handle his blatant lie. "Did you or did you not just throw that eraser across the room?"

Joe could see he had her backed in a corner. She had made the mistake of counting on an honest, obvious answer in order to rub his nose in his guilt. Phrasing her accusation as a question made her case rely on Joe's own testimony against himself. All he had to do was abandon the honesty she was counting on.

"No, I didn't."

You almost got the feeling he now believed his lie was truth. There was another brief pause as we all waited for the winner in this battle of wills.

"Okay, Joe, get back to work."

193

The heart is deceitful above all things and beyond cure. Who can understand it? I the Lord search the heart and examine the mind, to reward a man according to his conduct, according to what his deeds deserve. (Jeremiah 17:9-10)

I've lost touch with my friend Joe over the years. I hope he eventually came to grips with the destructive consequences of his deceitful heart. If not, I'm sure he's in a pathetic state, because you don't escape responsibility with deceit for very long. You just kid yourself into thinking you can build bluff upon bluff, and lie upon lie.

Joe's deceit had come full circle. He had convinced himself that the objective was to get through typing class with the minimum amount of commitment or work. He somehow missed the objective of learning to type. Joe's lack of responsibility, his arrogance, and his disobedience to our teacher flowed naturally from his wrong objective. He began by deceiving himself in his own heart. It was only natural that his self-deceit would eventually lead him to deceive others.

One of the most natural things in the world is to "follow your heart," to do what seems right to you. Then, when you get into trouble, you look within yourself for solutions to your problems.

Proverbs says that apart from God, the human heart is self-deceiving and hopeless. Its motives are selfish by nature, and it will tell us whatever seems self-serving at the time. When that destructive approach gets us into trouble, our sinful natural heart will lie and tell us we can figure our way out of our condition. We can't. And unless I miss my guess, Joe can't type either.

Did you throw the eraser? Well, did you?

Who are the people around you who are obviously following their own natural hearts rather than God? Is there any way you can help them recognize their delusion? Are there areas of your own life today where you've been kidding yourself about what's right when God has clearly said something else?

You might also take a look at ... Genesis 6:5; 1 Corinthians 4:4-5

*"Holding back" from
God is sort of like ...*

Spending Your
Savings Account

*Do you ever find yourself disobeying or holding back
from God for a really "good" reason? What motivates
you to do that?*

My first savings account started with a five dollar deposit.
It grew in size, largely because the adults in my life
took as great an interest in the account as I took in it
myself. Birthday gifts got larger. Earning money got easier. My
little passbook drew approving smiles and nods from everyone,
and each time I paraded in to make a deposit, I felt I was making
my parents, the bank teller, and the entire banking industry very,
very proud.

Then the baseball season rolled around. My two closest
friends got new baseball mitts, and I was struck with the realization that my own mitt was terribly worn and out of style. Suddenly the approval of the banking industry didn't seem quite so
important.

For several weeks I agonized over how to turn my bank account into a new baseball mitt with minimum adult disapproval.
I contemplated a "private" withdrawal without my parents'
knowledge. I considered "losing" my old mitt and pleading hardship with my mom and dad. Every solution I came up with,
however, involved a deceiving excuse, or an outright lie. Mean-
while the money, the approving nods, and the pennies and pennies of interest kept rolling in from people who assumed they
were helping finance my college education.

After an internal moral struggle greater than any eight-year-old should be asked to endure, I decided just to level with my dad. The world financial market would have to go on without my support. I needed a new baseball mitt.

My dad didn't completely hide his disappointment. In fact, I remember most of the points he made in his short speech on saving versus spending. But I give him a lot of credit for his attitude and his approach. In the end, he said it was my money and I could do with it as I pleased. My dad and I made peace over that decision. But to this day I remember the icy stare of the bank teller as he zeroed out my account.

> *Now a man named Ananias, together with his wife Sapphira, also sold a piece of property. With his wife's full knowledge he kept back part of the money for himself, but brought the rest and put it at the apostles' feet.*
>
> *Then Peter said, "Ananias, how is it that Satan has so filled your heart that you have lied to the Holy Spirit and have kept for yourself some of the money you received for the land? Didn't it belong to you before it was sold? And after it was sold, wasn't the money at your disposal? What made you think of doing such a thing? You have not lied to men but to God."*
>
> *When Ananias heard this, he fell down and died. And great fear seized all who heard what had happened.* (Acts 5:1-5)

I worried about and feared the icy stare of the bank teller for weeks before I withdrew my baseball mitt money. Sure, the money was mine, but I knew that withdrawing it meant trading off some of the prestige I had earned as a "junior banker." I wanted to have it both ways. And lying, it seemed, could help me do that.

Ananias probably thought of all sorts of "good reasons" for lying about the money he and his wife gave to the church. Peter made it clear that the money was his to do with as he pleased. His sin was wanting to "have it both ways," and therefore trying to hold back the truth from God.

I like to think that as a Christian I'm incapable of lying to God, or even to my family and friends. But wanting to please myself and please others at the same time can do funny things to my judgment, and that's when I'm most tempted to rationalize or lie. I think to myself, "If I can do one thing, and they can think I'm doing another and everybody's happy, what's the harm?" The harm is that lies create distrust, and distrust destroys relationships.

Sometimes being honest means choosing between what I want and what others will think of me. In my case, that choice gave me a baseball mitt at the expense of some adult approval. Whether my choice was the wisest one or not, it was at least made without the lies that so strongly tempted me. Ananias wasn't willing to make a choice between what he wanted and what others thought of him, and the resulting lie cost him his life. I guess the icy stare from the bank teller wasn't so bad after all.

How good are your excuses?

Are you avoiding obedience to God in any areas of your life today? What are your best excuses for doing so? Do any of those excuses approach lying to God about your motives? How could you get that situation right today?

You might also take a look at... Matthew 23:1-8; Mark 7:8-13

12

Peer pressure is sort of like...

A Mouthful of Toothpaste

Which people in your life carry the greatest influence over you? Is it a healthy influence, an unhealthy influence, or a mixture?

The house where I grew up during grade school had only one bathroom. So frequently my older brother Nevin and I found ourselves hurriedly getting ready for school at the same time, usually trying to spit in the same sink.

Maybe that's what motivated my brother's creativity on the morning he decided to enlighten me on tooth brushing. I had outraced him to the sink, and he was having to wait while I brushed. As I began to rinse out my mouth, he looked at me in disbelief and asked, "What are you doing?"

"Brushing my teeth!" I gurgled, wondering at the apparent stupidity of his question.

"You're not going to spit out the toothpaste, are you?" he continued. "If you spit out the toothpaste, it can't fight cavities as well! Everybody knows that. You have to leave it in there and swish it around your teeth until it all soaks in."

I like to think I exercised some initial skepticism and logical thinking in this matter, but the fact is that he convinced me my dental hygiene depended on following his advice. The next two weeks I left for school foaming at the mouth.

Fortunately, my mother eventually noticed the white ooze dripping from my chin as I headed out the door. She asked me what it was.

"Ftoofpastf!" I sputtered.

"Why didn't you rinse your mouth out?" she asked evenly, with a sort of I-know-my-son-isn't-as-stupid-as-he's-acting tone that always made me wince. I knew then that I had been had.

> *Andrew, Simon Peter's brother, was one of the two who heard what John had said and who had followed Jesus. The first thing Andrew did was to find his brother Simon and tell him, "We have found the Messiah" (that is, the Christ).*
> (John 1:40-41)

Brothers, I suppose, are the earliest and perhaps strongest version of peer pressure. All the elements are there. They're in the same social group: their family. They're trying to please the same audience: their parents. They're competing for the same prize: the privilege to lead and influence. Andrew and Peter probably knew the same brotherly peer pressure that my brother and I did.

Whether in a family or some other social group, there's an inevitable pressure to conform, to be like those in the group who have something or know something you don't. In my case, the idea that my brother knew a better way to brush teeth made me not want to be left behind in the tragedy of tooth decay. In Peter's case, the possibility that his brother may have met the Christ gave him a similar choice between being a skeptic or a follower.

Peer situations carry with them two avenues of responsibility. One peer has the responsibility of influencing wisely. The other has the responsibility of discerning when to follow and when to stand alone.

Andrew and Peter both carried out their peer responsibilities in the most positive way. My brother and I blew both ends of ours—but not always. It was my brother's profession of faith in Christ that one day encouraged me to do the same.

Are you brushing wisely?

How many of the peer situations you'll face today will be positive ones? How many will be potentially negative ones? How will you discern the difference? Are there peers you need to start steering clear of because they're not using their influence wisely? Do you have any peer influences that you need to handle more responsibly?

You might also take a look at . . . Genesis 27:1-40; Numbers 12:1-16

Following God is sort of like . . .

Crowd Breaking

Do the people around you encourage or discourage your Christian faith? How do you handle it when those around you challenge or ridicule what you believe?

My first year in college brought some big challenges to my faith in God. I guess that's not unusual. For many people, age eighteen or nineteen is a critical decision point in their spiritual life.

My critical decision point came at a time when I was seriously questioning the faith of my childhood and my parents. My new independence away at college gave me great freedom to do and think whatever I wanted. My professors encouraged an openness to all kinds of thinking, yet implied that religious belief meant you weren't thinking at all.

And then there were the crowds—the students in my classes, my roommate, the guys on my floor, the girls I was meeting, the basketball team—all the voices around me seemed to be saying that it was absurd to make God part of my life's equation.

In my first semester's sociology class, for example, the professor spoke matter-of-factly about how each culture "creates" its own gods after its own fears and unknowns. That made sense to me—as long as he was talking about pygmies in Africa creating gods of the forest. But surely we all agreed there was a true, living God, right? When I offered that comment in class, I was greeted with cool or sarcastic comments from my classmates and a patronizing response from the professor. As the semester went on, I realized how very alone this half-committed eighteen-year-old Christian was, and I felt my own faith beginning to slip, badly.

> As Jesus approached Jericho, a blind man was sitting by the roadside begging. When he heard the crowd going by, he asked what was happening. They told him, "Jesus of Nazareth is passing by."
>
> He called out, "Jesus, Son of David, have mercy on me!"
>
> Those who led the way rebuked him and told him to be quiet, but he shouted all the more, "Son of David, have mercy on me!"
>
> Jesus stopped and ordered the man to be brought to him. When he came near, Jesus asked him, "What do you want me to do for you?"
>
> "Lord, I want to see," he replied.
>
> Jesus said to him, "Receive your sight; your faith has healed you." Immediately he received his sight and followed Jesus, praising God. When all the people saw it, they also praised God. (Luke 18:35-42)

Everyone has crowds that try to shout down any act of faith. Throughout the Bible, "the crowd" is almost always antagonistic to those who would be faithful. The blind man in Jericho apparently knew of Jesus' Messianic reputation, for he called out to Jesus as the "Son of David." But the crowd, who found Jesus interesting, entertaining, even worth following for a while, was quick to disapprove when the blind man dared to call out to Jesus as God.

That's how my crowds were treating me and my feeble gestures of faith. "Sure, keep on whining, blind man," they seemed to be saying. "Not only don't we believe in God, we don't see your feeble faith making much of a difference in your life." Unfortunately, they were right. My weakly supported references to God must have been as absurd to my crowds as the blind man's cry was to his.

Fortunately, there was at least one faithful, mature believer in one of my crowds. He invited me to a Bible study where only a handful of students from campus gathered each week. It was there on perhaps the most pivotal night of my life that we studied this passage about Jesus and the blind man.

By God's amazing grace, I recognized that night that I had been waiting for Jesus to come and coax me into commitment like he seemed to do for Zacchaeus in the following chapter. But I suddenly saw that I was more like the blind man. I already knew Jesus was who he claimed to be. My need was to take that little morsel of faith and cry out to Jesus over the crowds of my life that I too needed my sight restored.

Overwhelmed with guilt and despair, I hurried out of the Bible study and roamed the dark college campus until after midnight. Knowing nothing else to do, I poured my heart out to God with passion my faith had never known before. Then, on a footbridge over the little river that ran through the campus, I agreed with God that he was more qualified to control my life than I was.

About 2:00 A.M., my sleepy father received a phone call from his sobbing son. Writing about it even now puts a lump in my throat. My dad and mom had been praying for my spiritual sight for quite a while, even when I was claiming not to be blind. I had to let them know the crowds hadn't won.

For me, spiritual rehabilitation meant transferring to a different college, getting re-established in God's Word, and plugging in to the support of a solid church. Even for the Christian, crowds don't just go away, and they continue to be a detracting part of my life. But by God's grace, they'll never shout my faith down again. I can see.

How loud is your crowd?

Who are the crowds that will attempt to shout down your faith today? Are you ready to cry all the louder over their stifling noise? Are there "good crowds" that could help strengthen your voice, and your faith?

You might also take a look at . . . Luke 23:13-25; Acts 17:5-9

Hypocrisy is sort of like . . .

Partying in the Wrong Basement

How deep does your Christianity go? Are there times when your faith is merely a thin coating over less honorable motives and behavior?

As I walked through the doorway of the unfamiliar house, I couldn't help but be a little nervous. It had taken some courage for me to attend this party, where I knew there were likely to be things going on that would be unwise or just plain wrong. But it was probably the most prestigious party I had ever been invited to, and as an up-and-coming sophomore in my high school's social ranks, I felt it was important for me to take advantage of opportunities like this. I was sure I could diplomatically make any moral stands I needed to, and simply exit the party if I got in over my head.

As I came around the corner at the bottom of the basement stairway, I saw Gail. At first I wasn't sure it was her because she looked different than she usually did at church. She was dressed differently than she usually was at church. And she was certainly acting differently than I'd ever imagined she could from knowing her at church.

You could tell she was just as uncomfortable seeing me as I was seeing her, especially in her present condition and position. She gave me a curt nod and awkward smile before turning away, and I decided to give her a break and go back upstairs. I left the party early, long before I'd really made any of the social headway that had been my motive and purpose for coming. But something had made me leery, almost afraid of spending time in that basement, and of who might come around the corner and remind me that I shouldn't be there.

> *My people come to you, as they usually do, and sit before you to listen to your words, but they do not put them into practice. With their mouths they express devotion, but their hearts are greedy for unjust gain.* (Ezekiel 33:31)

> *Do not conform any longer to the pattern of this world, but be transformed by the renewing of your mind. Then you will be able to test and approve what God's will is—his good, pleasing and perfect will.* (Romans 12:2)

God told the prophet Ezekiel that he shouldn't be surprised at the hypocrisy of his fellow countrymen. A disappointing number of people who appear to be following God are really pursuing some other agenda. Hundreds of years later, Paul would write to the church at Rome, urging them to avoid conformity and hypocrisy by constantly renewing and purifying their motives and innermost thoughts.

The night of that prestigious party, both Gail and I demonstrated that we had problems with our motives and innermost thoughts. As God said to Ezekiel, we both had hearts that were greedy for unjust gain. Each of us hoped to gain a reputation that we didn't deserve by pretending to be different things to different people.

Gail and I never talked about our basement encounter. As the weeks went by, she attended church less and less, and I attended questionable parties less and less. In the few brief seconds our eyes had met at that party, we had both found hypocrisy to be an uncomfortable facade to maintain.

Are you going to the right parties?

How many of your friends would be surprised to hear you're a Christian? How many of your Christian friends would be surprised by the parts of your daily life they don't see? What does "renewing your mind" mean, and how could it help transform your occasional double life into a more consistent life of faith? Have you renewed your mind yet today?

You might also take a look at... Matthew 23:25-27; Luke 14:26-33

DAY 81

Seeking God's will is sort of like...

Asking Freshmen the Right Question

Have you ever desperately wanted to know God's will about something, but not known how to find it? When God doesn't seem to be revealing his specific will to you, how do you pray?

It was the week before school started, and the day of freshman registration. As a junior, my classes were all set. But my dating life wasn't. Having broken up with a fairly long-term girlfriend over the summer, I was ready to come back to school for a fresh start. Maybe even a freshman start.

I had been burned in the past by getting a slow start on the dating scene. The previous year, half the freshman girls were already paired up with someone the first week of school. I was amazed at how that could happen when I hadn't even worked my way up to meeting any of them yet. This year, I decided, I needed a more aggressive approach.

I found it. As editor of the school newspaper for the coming year, I was able to get permission to come to freshman registration and set up an interview table. Positioned strategically between the class scheduling line and the book purchasing line, I was able to talk to each and every new freshman, "interviewing" them on whether they were able to schedule the classes they wanted.

Of course, the interviews with the girls took much longer than the interviews with the guys. And the interviews with the cute girls seemed to take even longer. Why? There was a totally different slate of questions for the cute girls. I didn't even ask the guys their names. Two or three quick yes/no questions and they were on their way. My interest in them was statistical, a means to an end.

My interest in the girls was different. Their questions had to do with who they were, what they liked, and most importantly, whether or not they were interested in working on the newspaper staff.

As he neared Damascus on his journey, suddenly a light from heaven flashed around him. He fell to the ground and heard a voice say to him, "Saul, Saul, why do you persecute me?"

"Who are you, Lord?" Saul asked.

"I am Jesus, whom you are persecuting," he replied. "Now get up and go into the city, and you will be told what you must do." (Acts 9:3-6)

Saul had just been knocked flat on his back by the One whose followers he had spent his life trying to destroy. Saul's zealous, tormented, almost possessed persecution of the church in God's name showed how desperately he desired to be in God's will. But to this point, whatever prayers he had been uttering, whatever questions he had been asking of God had evidently been misdirected. Only now, on the road to Damascus and in the presence of the Lord, did he come up with the right question. It was a question whose answer would reveal God's will for Saul and set him upon a course that would completely transform his life, as well as his name. He asked, "Who are you, Lord?"

I wonder if there's a better prayer anywhere than this four-word question. Perhaps Paul had been praying, "How can I stop the church?" or "Why are you letting these heretical followers of Jesus grow in number?" or "When will you let the Jewish people have the freedom and stature they deserve?" Finally, Jesus got his attention in a supernatural way, and it inspired the question God wanted to answer in Saul's life. The answer was that Jesus is God, and that Saul's worst enemy was about to become his best friend. Once the question of who Jesus wanted to be to Saul was answered, the next steps in the direction for his life could be revealed.

I've been told that my stunt in the freshman registration line that year was a devious, self-serving, underhanded way to meet girls. Actually, that criticism came mainly from the other upper-class guys who hadn't thought of it themselves. But I've never regretted creating that opportunity to ask the important "who are you?" question to those freshman girls. After all, the one I met in the line who did start working on the newspaper later became my wife.

What questions are you asking?

What are the questions you most often ask God when seeking his will? How often do you ask God to show you who he is and who he wants to be in your life? Do you have time today to simply ask God that question, and wait quietly for his Spirit's answer?

You might also take a look at . . . Exodus 3:1-14; Matthew 16:13-19

Beating the Clock, Not the Coach

Do you ever find yourself performing Christian service for the approval of someone other than God? Does the value of those things change at all?

A
t the end of one of our less successful basketball seasons, our frustrated coach latched onto a new zeal for conditioning. He announced that at the beginning of the next season, everyone on the team would be required to run a timed mile in five minutes and fifteen seconds. If we weren't as competitive as we'd like to be with the teams in our league, he reasoned, at least we'd be in the best shape.

I didn't know how fast I could run a mile. I'm not sure I'd ever tried to run a mile. I'm quite sure I'd never had any desire to run a mile. So three months before the new season started, I introduced a mile run into my morning routine. I figured that was plenty of time to meet the goal he'd set. After a month of chugging through my neighborhood, however, I was still wheezing back into my front yard in just over six minutes.

I redoubled my efforts over the next few weeks, and gradually got my time down to within fifteen or twenty seconds of the required standard. But the deadline date came far too soon, and as I positioned myself at the starting line for my twenty laps around the gymnasium, I knew I'd have to count on a heavy adrenalin dose to produce my best time ever.

I still smile at my former coach's sense of the dramatic. He and I were the only ones in the gym—no teammates, no cheerleaders, no audience. He plugged in the scoreboard clock, and set it for five minutes and fifteen seconds. If I didn't finish my twenty laps in that amount of time, the loud honk in an empty gym would mock my failure.

In the first few laps of that critical race, I sought motivation for my performance in several wrong places. I focused my attention on the cones that marked my difficult course. I focused my attention on the bench and tried to imagine the support of my teammates. I focused my attention on the bleachers and tried to muster an image of the home crowd and cheerleaders that would glorify my efforts in the coming season. About halfway through the race, I focused my attention on the coach that had concocted this harebrained conditioning thing, and imagined different ways to blow up his car.

> *While all the people were listening, Jesus said to his disciples, "Beware of the teachers of the law. They like to walk around in flowing robes and love to be greeted in the marketplaces and have the most important seats in the synagogues and the places of honor at banquets. They devour widows' houses and for a show make lengthy prayers. Such men will be punished most severely."* (Luke 20:45-47)

Your motive in doing something has a great deal to do with the value of doing it. There's great danger and judgment, Jesus says, in pretending to do things for God when I'm really doing them for the approval of others or the benefits to myself.

When I act like a Christian to impress my friends, that's like running the race for the applause of the crowd. When I act like a Christian to please my parents, or even my pastor, that's like running the race for praise from the coach. Even when I act like a Christian to feel good about myself, I've settled for an inferior motive. That's like running the race just to prove I could do it.

It's not that any of those motives are evil in and of themselves, but they all fall short of the real reason for living a consistent Christian life. They all turn my eyes away from the true standard—the Lord Jesus whom I seek to honor with my life's race.

Have you guessed yet where my gaze ended up during that mile run? After I tore my eyes away from being bitterly fixed on my coach, I turned with determination to the clock. It was my real standard. It would be the true and final judge of my performance in this race. And as the buzzer went off—two seconds after I crossed the finish line—I knew I had run the race with perseverance, and I sat down there on the gym floor in a place of great honor. After all, that's what Jesus did after he finished his race.

Who are you running for?

Who or what do you find competes the most for your attention as you run the race of faith? What effect are those distractions having? What steps could you take today to fix your eyes on Jesus as you act out your faith?

You might also take a look at ... 1 Corinthians 3:11-15; Hebrews 12:2

DAY 83

Perseverance is sort of like ...

Walking in a Blizzard

Do you ever find yourself "turning back" to the way things were before you came to know God personally? Why can the old ways seem inviting, even after you've tasted the new way?

The basketball game was over, and I was standing outside the locker room waiting for my teammates to finish showering. The home team had won again. Unfortunately, we were the visiting team. Through the glass doors of the gym, I could see our two vans warming up to take us on the long, two-hour drive home. It was snowing hard, but I noticed only one of the vans had its windshield wipers running. Then our coach came in from outside, stomping snow off his feet and dusting off the quarter inch of powder that had quickly accumulated on his hood.

"We're not going anywhere tonight," he announced with a tone of disgust left over from his halftime speech to us. The water pump had gone out on one of the vans. We'd have to spend the night and try to get it fixed in the morning.

"I can take a couple of guys with me if you want me to, Coach." It was Scott, a former teammate who had graduated a year ago. He had driven down with his girlfriend for the game and was getting ready to head out into the blizzard in his little compact car.

"I'll go, Coach!" I managed to blurt out a split second ahead of several other volunteers. None of us savored the thought of spending the night there. Before long we were in the backseat of Scott's little car, battling what had become a pretty substantial blizzard on a stretch of barren country road. We were about a half hour up the highway when his engine froze up and decided to hibernate for good.

As we sat in that frozen car, I was amazed that there was literally no traffic on the road at all. The snow was already almost a foot thick, and we couldn't see more than ten feet in front of us. I remember thinking that we were in real danger. People had frozen to death in better circumstances than these. We looked around nervously at one another, then voted to start walking. We were only a few hundred yards up the road before we started arguing over whether to turn back to the car.

I am astonished that you are so quickly deserting the one who called you by the grace of Christ and are turning to a different gospel—which is really no gospel at all. Evidently some people are throwing you into confusion and are trying to pervert the gospel of Christ. (Galatians 1:6-7)

During the first half hour that we hoofed it through that blizzard, we debated strongly whether we were doing the right thing. We didn't know how long it was to the next place of warmth. We didn't know exactly where we were. We were dressed up to attend a ball game, not cross Antarctica. Two things kept us walking forward: the hope that safety lay before us, and the certainty that turning back to the car possibly meant death.

That's the spirit, really, of Paul's exhortation to the Galatian church. The going had gotten tough, and some had decided that going back to the laws and legalism of Judaism was better than walking the difficult road of faith in Christ. Paul's warning is clear and gets even more urgent as the passage continues. However uncertain or difficult depending on Christ may get, turning back to where they were before was much worse. Persevere in your faith, Paul urged, if not for the seeming uncertainty of what you see ahead, for the absolute certainty of what lies behind.

When we walked into the truck stop restaurant forty-five minutes later, my previously wet hair was literally frozen into a helmet of ice. My extremities were numb, and I could barely talk until my face muscles thawed out. But I was infinitely happier to be in that truck stop than back in the little frozen car that was dead on the highway.

Going back to the car?

Which parts of your walk of faith are you quickest to turn back from when things get tough? Is it fear of what lies ahead or the apparent comfort of what lies behind that gets to you? What part of that tough walk might God want you to persevere through today?

You might also take a look at ... Exodus 16:1-4; Hebrews 3:12-13

Worship is sort of like ...

Sunday Trips to the Dairy Queen

Is Sunday any different from the other days of the week? Is it only different if you're a Christian?

From the house where I grew up, you could walk out the back door, down the alley a half block, and then across the street to the local Dairy Queen. I can remember many summer nights when we'd barely finish dinner before I would ask my dad for "DQ money." By the time the dishes had been cleared from the table, I could be back with a tray of assorted ice cream treats for the whole family.

But never on Sundays. As a pastor, my dad felt that it was important for us to set an example for the community that said Sunday was special. Sunday should be a day of worship and rest, he taught us. That meant we shouldn't buy things we didn't absolutely need, so we didn't contribute to anyone else's having to work on Sunday. I really missed the old DQ on summer Sundays. But deep down, I admired my dad for taking such a principled stand.

That's why I found what happened about ten years later so hard to understand. By then we had moved to the suburbs of a major city, and my little brother who was barely old enough to gum ice cream from the old DQ was now ready to start his first part-time job at a local drug store. He was low man on the totem pole, and as a result was asked to work Sundays. To my amazement, my dad agreed. I wanted to sue him for five hundred and twenty Sundays worth of sundaes.

Remember the Sabbath day by keeping it holy. Six days you shall labor and do all your work, but the seventh day is a Sabbath to the Lord your God. On it you shall not do any work, neither you, nor your son or daughter, nor your manservant or maidservant, nor your animals, nor the alien within your gates. For in six days the Lord made the heavens and the earth, the sea, and all that is in them, but he rested on the seventh day. Therefore the Lord blessed the Sabbath day and made it holy. (Exodus 20:8-11)

Then he said to them, "The Sabbath was made for man, not man for the Sabbath. So the Son of Man is Lord even of the Sabbath." (Mark 2:27-28)

Any commandment can become distorted if it's only followed by the letter without giving attention to its intent. Most of us could recite, "Remember the Sabbath day by keeping it holy," and perhaps most of the other nine commandments as well. But how many of us could recite the three verses after this fourth commandment? It's there that we find God's heart and his mind in establishing the Sabbath day as holy.

God created within us a need for both worship and rest. He didn't need either one when he finished creating the world, but he chose to model them for us by setting aside as special the seventh day of each week. Why? His intent and desire was that we regularly pause from our labor and routine to worship him as the creator of all things.

I still kid my dad about the apparent discrepancy between his DQ rule when I was a boy and his flexibility in accepting my brother's work schedule. But my dad tends to run just slightly ahead of me in his thinking about things such as this, and I've come to understand his explanation for the apparent change of colors. He had become less and less concerned with legalistic avoidance of work on Sunday and more concerned that my little brother have a regular cycle of rest and worship for both his physical and spiritual health. Those had not been compromised by my brother's work schedule.

There are those who still argue for Sunday's particular sanctity and for a more strict observance of workless rest on that day. I still lean that way myself, within reason. At the same time, I've come to realize that losing track of a commandment's intent and allowing it to become a thoughtless ritual is a lot more dangerous than a little ice cream, even on Sunday.

Having a sundae this Sunday?

How many of the Bible's commandments do you obey blindly, without fully understanding their background or intent? Is that all bad? Do you think studying the Ten Commandments for their deepest intent would make them easier to follow or harder? What kind of adjustment could you make this week that would help make Sunday holy in the way God really intended?

You might also take a look at . . . Leviticus 23:3; 1 Corinthians 16:2

Prayer is sort of like . . .

Knowing the President's Phone Number

Does the attitude you have as you come to God in prayer affect the way you end up praying? How would you describe the way you most often approach God in prayer?

Who's the most famous, important, influential person you know? Do you know him or her personally, or have you just met or seen the person from a distance? I don't mean to brag, but I have the phone number of the president of the United States. I also have the phone numbers of the pope, the president of Russia, and the queen of England.

Impressed? Don't be. I don't know any of those people personally. I got their phone numbers on a card in a piece of junk mail. At the top of the card was the headline: "Five Very Important Phone Numbers." After the four genuinely important phone numbers was the number of the company that sent the mailing.

At the time I rolled my eyes at the obvious gimmick, but I have to admit it made me smile. I was amused at the cleverness of the promotional idea, but more than that I was sort of pleased at the idea of having those phone numbers in my possession. It's not that I thought any of those people would actually answer the phone if I called. The best I could hope for beyond a recording or a busy signal was to get through to a receptionist or operator who had probably never even met the big boss.

Still, I valued the phone numbers. A small part of me believed that if I called on the right day, talked to the right middleman, caught the right number of people in the right mood, asked the right question, I might actually talk to the president or the queen. That's probably why I've never called the numbers. I don't want my distant hope or fantasy to be dashed by hearing an impersonal recording instead of an important voice. So I never call. But I still have the numbers.

> *Therefore, brothers, since we have confidence to enter the Most Holy Place by the blood of Jesus, by a new and living way opened for us through the curtain, that is, his body, and since we have a great priest over the house of God, let us draw near to God with a sincere heart in full assurance of faith, having our hearts sprinkled to cleanse us from a guilty conscience and having our bodies washed with pure water.*
> (Hebrews 10:19-22)

Before Jesus came to earth and died, the average person had less hope of getting through personally to God than I have of getting through personally to the president. An elite priesthood and a complicated system of sacrifices and rituals stood between each of God's children and the austere Holy of Holies. Once a year the high priest would pass through the thick curtain that separated mere humans from the inner sanctuary of the temple. A rope would be tied around his ankles so that his dead body could be recovered if God chose to strike him dead. There the high priest would offer a blood sacrifice for the sins of the people, who could only wait outside, hoping that their representative had successfully communicated with God on their behalf.

How flippantly and presumptuously I often approach God. It's not that I should come to prayer with the same fear and trembling that characterized the people of the Old Testament. Jesus' death on the cross tore the curtain in two, and I no longer depend on a high priest or an animal sacrifice to represent me. I come freely, joyfully, boldly, because the blood of Jesus has given me "a new and living way" into God's presence.

When I think of what once separated people like me from almighty God, it makes me want to value my privilege of prayer much, much more than the phone numbers on my silly card. When I think about the amazing fact that God always answers his line personally and Jesus pays the long distance bill, it makes me wish I called more often and talked longer.

You have the number, don't you?

Do you consider prayer more like calling the president or calling your best friend? Is there value in both attitudes? Do you ever approach God with an attitude that treats him as less than who he is? How will you approach him today?

You might also take a look at . . . Matthew 27:50-54; Ephesians 2:12-22

Intercession is sort of like . . .

Praying for Johnny Carson

Do you pray for anyone who's not a family member or friend? Why do you pray for them?

I pray for Johnny Carson. Without exception, everyone I've ever told that has laughed. At first, they're sure I'm joking, or that there's some punch line or explanation I'm not telling them. When they see that I'm serious, they often ask something even more incredible than the statement I've just made. They ask, "Have you met him?"

I haven't met him. Odds are I'll never have a chance to meet him. I did attend the "Tonight Show" starring Johnny Carson one time before Johnny retired, but Jay Leno was the guest host that night. No, I always reply, I haven't met him.

"Did something happen to him?" is usually the next question to follow. "Is he sick?"

I guess that's a logical question. If there's one singular reason we Christians seem comfortable interceding, it's that someone is ill or having surgery. It's a very non-threatening sort of thing to pray about someone else's gallstones. Praying for the physical can often be easier than praying for the spiritual.

I usually have to confess to my interrogator that I'm not up-to-date on Johnny's physical condition. He might be sick, but no one called me about it. That's not why I pray for him. By this time, most everyone just gives up and asks, "Why on earth do you pray for Johnny Carson?"

> *Brothers, my heart's desire and prayer to God for the Israelites is that they may be saved. For I can testify about them that they are zealous for God, but their zeal is not based on knowledge.* (Romans 10:1-2)

In Paul's letter to the church at Rome, he spoke of his "heart's desire and prayer." It was that his own people, the ones most like him, might be saved. Even though Paul's main mission and ministry was to the non-Jewish peoples of the world, he had a zealous, passionate concern for the Israelites.

Paul saw the good in his people—that they were genuinely "zealous for God." He saw the potentially tragic need of his people—that "their zeal is not based on knowledge." Perhaps most importantly, Paul saw himself in his people. He knew he had been in the same condition before God's grace came into his life.

I don't know Johnny Carson's personal spiritual condition. The only picture I have of him is through the window of a television screen or the pages of a newspaper or magazine. But through all those windows, I've never heard him profess to have a personal relationship with Jesus Christ.

So I pray for him. Why? I like him. I relate to him. I see a lot of me in him. I guess a lot of America does—that's why he's been such a success in show business. In many ways, I'd love to

be in his position. At the same time, I know the world in which he lives has very few opportunities for godly influence and that his wealth and success could be blinding to him—they would be to me.

Amidst all these thoughts, I can't help but imagine and fantasize about the influence someone like Johnny could have if his life were yielded to God. Then I remember that God tends to use the seemingly insignificant and weak to carry out his purposes, lest there be any confusion about the source of power. So I go back to praying for Johnny in the same way and for the same reasons Paul prayed for Israel. He reminds me of me before I knew God personally.

Are you praying for the lifestyles of the rich and famous?

Do you admire a famous or celebrity "hero" who doesn't appear to have a personal relationship with God? In what ways might it be good for you to pray for someone like that? Could it even be good for the person for whom you pray? Who will you pray for "from a distance" today?

You might also take a look at . . . Job 42:10; Colossians 1:9-12

Living for God is sort of like . . .

Playing Well at the Wrong End of the Court

Do you ever wonder why God put you where he did?
Does the difficulty of your circumstances sometimes
make you wonder if you're out of God's will?

A s I stood in the high school gym among a hundred other freshman, I realized I might be making a mistake even trying out for the basketball team. After all, we had just moved to this huge city from a small town. The competition here was obviously much stiffer.

Sure, I had "started" on my junior high team back home, but this room was full of guys who had started at five or six different junior highs, all of them several times larger than mine. Some of them looked like they had spent several years there. I began to wonder if I had any kind of a chance, or if my highest goal shouldn't just be to get out of there without being embarrassed. Then the coaches made it worse.

"If you played at one of the following junior highs, please step down to this end of the court," the head coach droned in a heartless monotone, as if this part of the tryouts were nothing more than a boring formality. "Everyone else go down to the other end of the court, where Coach Purgatory will work with you for a while."

Okay, Purgatory wasn't really the assistant coach's name, but it might as well have been. He was obviously taking the "not good enough" players out of the way so the head coach could evaluate the proven players. The head coach then read off a list of local junior highs that, of course, didn't include mine.

I wanted to speak up and ask if I was an exception. I wanted to tell him that I had played before and deserved at least a chance to play at the end of the court where the true evaluation was going to take place. But I was afraid to say anything that presumed I even had a right to be there. Dutifully, I followed the assistant coach and forty other nobodies to the far end of the court—the wrong end of the court as far as hope of making the basketball team.

You are the light of the world. A city on a hill cannot be hidden. Neither do people light a lamp and put it under a bowl. Instead they put it on its stand, and it gives light to everyone in the house. In the same way, let your light shine before men, that they may see your good deeds and praise your Father in heaven. (Matthew 5:14-16)

Jesus uses a clear image to describe how those who live by faith are to penetrate the dark world around them. Our faith is to shine boldly, brightly. We are to be unafraid of calling attention to ourselves, as long as we're ready to redirect that attention to God when it comes. There's no reason to lack confidence. There's no reason to cower under a bowl of low self-esteem. If the light doesn't shine, we have no impact.

When I arrived on the "wrong end of the court," I made a decision that became one of my personal life commitments from that point forward. I decided that I would do my very best wherever I was asked to perform. I knew it might be the last time I played organized basketball. I knew that my best might not bring me the results I wanted. But I remember telling God that he was going to see my best that night, even if no one else was looking.

That decision was, and continues to be, one of the most liberating, empowering decisions I've ever made. Free from others' expectations and limited judgments, I relaxed and played my heart out. I stole one pass, then two, then three for breakaway lay ups. I saw Coach Purgatory's eyes light up. Then I made a couple of outside shots. I noticed the coaches conferring and looking my way.

One more steal, and I was invited to come play at the other end of the court. My light was shining, and they had noticed my good works. All that was left was giving God the credit. And I did.

Got a light?

Does a lack of confidence ever tempt you to quit or remain anonymous rather than shine the light of your faith? Would the motivation of giving God the glory change your attitude or your willingness to risk? Is there a "bowl" covering your light that you could remove today to show others you're living for God?

You might also take a look at... Acts 20:17-24; Ephesians 5:8-21

A healthy self-image is sort of like...

Hanging on the Refrigerator Door

On a scale of one to ten, how do you feel about yourself today? Is how you feel about yourself something you can control?

I'm not an artist. I admire people who can draw or paint or sculpt—as a matter of fact, I admire people who can color with crayons and stay between the lines—but I've never had much skill in that area.

In fact, one of my most traumatic academic experiences was during the second grade when I received a fairly low grade in art. Actually, art that year consisted of finishing one thematic coloring book each month. I was just a little too perfectionistic and thorough, and was always struggling just to finish my coloring book.

One month I couldn't get through all the turkeys, pilgrims, fall foliage, and cornucopias. The low grade I received for that period wasn't as stinging as the teacher's critique of my artistic ability on my report card: "Needs a faster crayon or a shorter coloring book."

I did better on snowmen and Santa the next month. But my artistic struggle continued. Every picture I made in Sunday school looked like a commentary on Genesis 1:2, where the earth is described as formless and empty. Every craft I did at school ended up looking like an ash tray. Even my Play-Doh didn't want to play with me.

It was demoralizing to bring home something I'd drawn or made and always have to explain what it was to my parents—especially the pictures I'd drawn of them. But I never hesitated to bring the stuff home. Why? Because it was always good enough for the refrigerator door.

> *For it is by grace you have been saved, through faith—and this not from yourselves, it is the gift of God—not by works, so that no one can boast. For we are God's workmanship, created in Christ Jesus to do good works, which God prepared in advance for us to do.* (Ephesians 2:8-10)

I guess I always knew that my art projects had little intrinsic worth or value. That's why our refrigerator door was so important to me. No matter what I brought home, and no matter what it looked like, my parents always displayed my work proudly there. I always thought that Mom and Dad just had poor taste. Only now, as a father, am I beginning to understand that what goes on the refrigerator door is valuable not for its own sake, but for the sake of the one who made it.

You and I are good enough to hang on God's refrigerator door. The Bible says we are his "workmanship." We are creatures saved by grace who come to the refrigerator door not as deserving art, but as a gift from the Son to the Father.

As long as I try to feel good about myself or my accomplishments on my own, I'm going to feel pretty ugly and worthless.

Even if my efforts are pretty good by others' standards—well, there are plenty of professional artists whose work would never have qualified for my folks' refrigerator door. It's only when I realize my worth as Christ's own new creation, a piece of art that he is shaping with his own hands, that I know and feel true value. I don't have to finish my coloring book. So there.

How do you draw the line?

Do you feel more like your own workmanship these days, or like God's? What's the difference between the two? Why do you think the Ephesians passage says we're not saved by good works, then says we were created in Christ Jesus to do them? Have you been feeling too high or too low about yourself, based on the wrong criteria? How could you correct that today?

You might also take a look at . . . Genesis 1:26-27; 2 Corinthians 5:16-21

DAY 89

Healthy dating is sort of like . . .

A Hayride with Judy

How do you go about getting to know someone in a dating relationship? Have you thought through your standards about how fast and how far you'll go when you date?

Everyone I know either vividly remembers their first real kiss, or is eagerly looking forward to it. I remember a college retreat where we were playing some sort of "truth or dare" type game, and the question that came up was "When was your first real kiss?" It was a relatively shy girl that was asked the question, and it made her pause nervously. She was sitting next to a similarly shy guy, but everyone in the room knew they were more than a little interested in each other.

"Let's see," she repeated the question thoughtfully to stall for more time, "when was my first real kiss..." There was a dramatic pause and a hush in the room that must have made her would-be boyfriend forget his shyness as he turned toward her.

"It could be right now, baby," he blurted out, then realized that his great one-liner was a little too close to his true feelings. He turned several shades of deeply embarrassed red. She matched his color and buried her face in her hands as the whole room filled with laughter.

The question, however, made us all think about that magical, memorable moment in our own lives. For me it was while I was in seventh grade, on the back of a hayride wagon. Judy, the cute little red-headed girl whose lips were my "first," had invited half our class out to her parents' farm for what promised to be THE social event of the school year. Weeks ahead of time, everyone was talking about the great opportunity to "make out."

I personally was approaching the event with some fear. I had never "made out" before, and didn't even know Judy very well. Maybe things are different now, but when I was in the seventh grade, you could spend most of a school year "liking" someone or even "going with" someone without ever having to talk to her or him much. But I stepped up to the challenge like a true macho guy. During that two-hour hayride, I kissed her—right on the mouth—not once, not twice, but three whole times.

When I came to school the Monday following the hayride, I felt I had fully matured into manhood. With three, count 'em, three kisses under my belt, I considered myself sexually active. That's when I started hearing the reports—real or fabricated—of how other couples had spent those two hours in the hay.

Flee from sexual immorality. All other sins a man commits are outside his body, but he who sins sexually sins against his own body. Do you not know that your body is a temple of the Holy Spirit, who is in you, whom you have received from God? You are not your own; you were bought at a price.

Therefore honor God with your body. (1 Corinthians 6:18-20)

God created us humans with a personality (the Bible sometimes calls it a soul), a spirit, and a body. He's designed us to get to know each other pretty much in that order. We get acquainted by exchanging our personalities in conversation. Occasionally we develop friendships deep enough to share matters of our spirit. Then, when our personalities and spirits intertwine with one another in deep, committed love, we may choose to express that love with our bodies.

Unfortunately, we tend to reverse or twist God's plan until we do just the opposite. We somehow think that by getting acquainted physically, we'll get to know each other more fully. It doesn't work that way. God owns and inhabits the bodies of his children as his temple, and he says that our sexuality is a gift for expressing love in a relationship, not a pleasureful playground for trying to find it.

It truly amazed me that kids my age had done—or even knew how to do—the things they said they'd done on that hayride. I had practically died of embarrassment putting my lips up against the lips of a girl whom I barely knew. I found out that I was in the minority as far as how I chose to get acquainted with my girlfriend. But I've never been sorry for how I used God's body that night.

How are you using your kisser?

Has your body ever gotten ahead of your soul and spirit in a relationship? Have you found yourself more interested in a relationship's physical progress than its spiritual progress? If you're not currently dating, are there commitments and decisions you could make now that won't be as easy to make later? If you are dating now, are you and God pleased with how you're planning to use his body?

You might also take a look at... Deuteronomy 13:6-8; Song of Songs 3:5

Sin is sort of like...

Cheating at Basketball

Is all disobedience to God the same, or do you find that sin takes different forms at different times? Is sin "trying hard and just not making it" or is it deliberately doing what's wrong?

As I ran out onto the gym floor to warm up for the basketball game, I felt pretty good. We hadn't had an outstanding season, but tonight's opponent was one of the weaker teams we'd play all year. They had a couple of big, burly guys that looked like they'd been in high school a few years longer than average, but they weren't generally a very fast or skilled team.

As I looked down toward their end of the gym, I noticed one of the big guys was looking at me. In fact, by the time my eyes met his, I got the feeling he had been looking at me for a while. His teammates were passing him up in line as he just stood there, staring at me.

I started to look away, but then he pointed to me and mouthed something. Instinctively, I checked to make sure everything was zipped or tied or laced or whatever on my uniform. Finding everything in order, I looked back to make sure he was

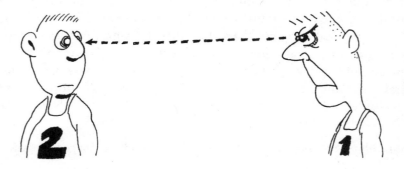

talking to me. He was. This time I could understand what he was saying. To paraphrase for the sake of civility, he said the equivalent of "You're mine."

I shook off his juvenile, macho intimidation attempt with a look of disgust, and thought to myself, We'll see what happens when the game starts—and we did. The first time down the floor, he was bumping and elbowing me, though discreetly enough to avoid detection by the referee. Then, the first time the ball was to be thrown in from out of bounds under our basket, he lined up just behind me and pulled about five hairs out of my leg.

I was aghast. Had he just done what I thought he had done? Reflexively, I turned and gave him a big "don't-pull-the-hairs-out-of-my-leg, buddy" shove. The referee called a foul on me. A couple of minutes later, he pulled on the bottom of my shorts. I shoved him again. I was called for another foul. By that time I had some idea of what he was trying to accomplish, and stopped retaliating. But the whole game he had me frazzled, and eventually the coach had to bench me so I could cool off and regain my composure.

> *Blessed is he whose transgressions are forgiven, whose sins are covered. Blessed is the man whose sin the Lord does not count against him and in whose spirit is no deceit.* (Psalm 32:1-2)

In these short verses about how great it is to be forgiven, the psalmist uses four different Hebrew words to describe sin. All four can be illustrated using basketball analogies:

1. Transgression is like stepping out of bounds. It's trespassing into forbidden territory. There are clear boundaries for a basketball game, and when a player steps out of bounds with the ball, his team is penalized.

2. Sin is like an "air ball." It's falling short of the mark, missing the basket entirely. Shooting an air ball is one of the most humbling experiences a basketball player can have. Believe me, I know.

3. The third word translated sin or iniquity means to twist or distort. It would be like a player on the other team calling you by

name and saying, "Throw me the ball." I've had that one happen too. It's pretty humiliating when it works.

4. Finally, deceit or guile is what my clever opponent was using on me. It's a deliberate decision to corrupt or do what's wrong. Usually using pretense or trickery, it's an attitude that says, "I ought to foul. I can get away with it."

While that dishonest player's approach was initially one of deceit, I also spent a lot of that game stepping out of bounds, shooting air balls, and throwing to the wrong person. They were all imperfections in my game, mistakes in my performance that began with a dishonest player's distractions, then multiplied as I played his game. I have a feeling Satan is one tough basketball player.

Are you letting The Cheater get to you?

Which description of sin do you most often find yourself tangled in: stepping out of bounds, falling short of the goal, twisting the truth, or deliberately deceiving? Does one ever consistently lead to the other? How could understanding these realities of sin help you be more ready to combat them today?

You might also take a look at... Romans 6:1-14; 1 John 3:4-10

Living for God is sort of like... **DAY 91**

A Mountain Path Overlooking the Interstate

Does the decision to live consistently for God get easier or harder as life goes on? Are there many people around you who are choosing to truly live for God?

When Beth and I finally saved enough money to "go see Europe," we were determined to see it up close and personal. So we abandoned the notions of tour groups and package deals, and set out to do it on our own. With no advance lodging reservations or specific advance plans, we picked up our rent-a-car in Holland and drove off to see ten countries in twenty-three days. Armed with a couple of maps, a travel book on Europe, and my French textbook from college, we were sure we could handle whatever we ran into in this quaint little continent.

As long as we were on the expressways, we did pretty well. In fact, things looked a lot like home. The fast-paced German "autobahn," in particular, was a lot of fun. I could be driving eighty-five miles per hour in the right lane, and get passed like I was standing still.

It was a little confusing, though. It seemed that everywhere we went we came across signs with arrows pointing to Ausfahrt. I was getting a kick out of the name, and told Beth it would be a fun place to go let off some steam. But even though the signs were all over Germany, we could never find the place on the map. Finally, the entrance to a parking garage gave us the education we needed in the German language. Einfahrt means "entrance." Ausfahrt simply means "exit." No wonder it was all over the expressway but not on the map.

It was that kind of limited understanding that eventually got us lost in Switzerland. Having visited a little mountain town, we were trying to get back to the expressway. But there were no Ausfahrts to be found. As Beth turned the map first this way, then that, I found myself on a side street, then a cobblestone street, then a gravel road, then a dirt road going up a mountain. The further we went, the fewer cars and people we saw.

Finally, I pulled the car to a stop and breathed a sigh of frustration. Out Beth's window I saw a Swiss yodeler and a mountain goat in the distance. Out my side, far in the distance down the mountain, I saw the expressway.

Enter through the narrow gate. For wide is the gate and broad is the road that leads to destruction, and many enter through it. But small is the gate and narrow the road that leads to life, and only a few find it. (Matthew 7:13-14)

Jesus described the "road that leads to life" like the mountain path we wandered up—narrow, obscure, and hard to find. By contrast, the "road that leads to destruction" is like the expressway—wide, crowded, and easy to get onto. He says enter through the narrow gate, even though the path is tougher and the company fewer.

The choice not to live for God is a wide gate—an Einfahrt if you will—to the world's expressway. Access is easy because you do whatever you want. You have great freedom to drive at high speeds, because everyone's getting away with whatever's right in their own eyes. That's why the expressway is fun. That's why it's so crowded. That's why its crashes are fatal.

The choice to live for God is a narrow gate—a mountain path whose hardship is real, but whose scenery is awesome and rare. Access is difficult, though not limited, because it demands that you deny rather than indulge yourself. Progress on the mountain path is sometimes slow, because the road itself is narrow. Each move must be deliberate, each misstep can lead to a dangerous fall. There aren't a lot of travelers on the mountain path, for it takes commitment to follow the narrow trail and to value where it leads, especially when the expressway is in plain sight.

How's your mountain driving?

Does your walk with God feel like a careful walk along a mountain path? Or do you seem to be flying along so fast on the expressway that the narrow path seems far away? Might you find an Ausfahrt on your expressway today that leads back eventually to the small gate and the narrow road?

You might also take a look at . . . Matthew 16:24-27; Luke 14:25-33